Simon Cutts

The Small Press Model

Uniformbooks

First published 2023
Copyright © Simon Cutts
All rights reserved

Photo acknowledgements: cover, Stephen Fareham; p.20, 91, William Allen Word & Image, London; p.32, Tom Phillips; p.53, Paul Etienne Lincoln; p.82, Erica Van Horn; p.84, Grainger Museum, University of Melbourne; p.86, Martha Kirwan; p.101, Artcurial, Paris; p.118, Clay Culbert; p.122-123, Getty Research Institute, Los Angeles; p.126, Southampton Art Gallery; p.139, 140, Reinhard Mucha, Galerie Max Hetzler.

ISBN 978-1-910010-34-1

Uniformbooks
7 Hillhead Terrace, Axminster, Devon EX13 5JL
uniformbooks.co.uk

Trade distribution in the UK by Central Books
centralbooks.com

Printed and bound by T J Books, Padstow, Cornwall

Synthesis   9

The Small Press Model

  The Collective Work in the Critical Mode   19
  Ian Hamilton Finlay's Wild Hawthorn Press   29
  The South Bank Show   31
  The Metaphor Books   35
  Threads in Relationship to Kettle's Yard   52
  Notes on The Unpainted Landscape   54
  Allotment   60
  The Presence of Landscape   62
  The Vinyl Project   63
  Certain Trees   65
  The Norfolk Years   70
  Construction Storage Despatch   77
  Made in English   82
  At Last   83
  Living and Publishing in Tipperary   86
  Locations   87

Equivalent Spaces

  On the flapability of the pamphlet   89
  A Concertina of Concertinas   89
  Typewriter Art   90
  To Climb Through A Hole in A Postcard   90
  The Format of the Small Shop   92
  Liable To Be Anywhere   95
  The Poem Itself   96
  The Small Publishers Fair   98
  A Case for Books   98

Particular Dislocations

Brancusi's Sewing Box	101
The Rain Paintings of Stephen Skidmore	102
The Two Stephens	105
Some Lacunae in Relationship to Brian Lane	107
Anglophone Digressions	109
Ian Gardner	111
In the Shadow of Bill Culbert	113
Working with Roger Ackling	119
A History of the Airfields of Lincolnshire	121
Some Notes on 'Affinity'	121
The Clustered Hang	126
Martin-pêcheur	126
The Pencils of Matsutani	131
Pangaea	132
Starting from Home	133
Notes on the work of Sol LeWitt	134
The Material Language of Carl Andre	135
Drinking Sculpture	136
The Vertical Earth Kilometer	137
Unique Forms of Continuity in Space	138
Wartesaal	139

Coracle Bibliography 142

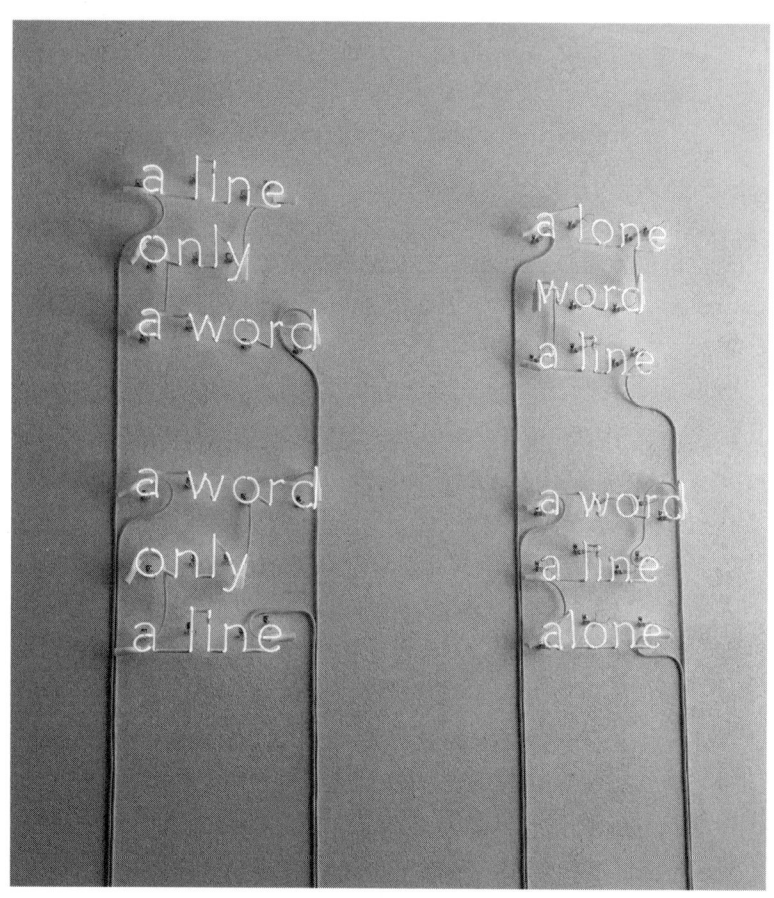

a line only a word, Beinecke Rare Book & Manuscript Library, 2018.

Synthesis

Small Press activity arises from the need and resolve for a critical alternative to mainstream publishing. It is a search for its own methods of producing and making available, and at the same time a discovery and awareness of the ways others have contributed to the field.

From the 'little magazine' of poetry publishing, it often begins with writing and leads to individual publications and books, together with accompanying printed ephemera of an often unclassifiable nature: having discovered the means of production, it is possible to improvise and delight in the extensions of the idea of publication.

With this collection of writings, I am trying to group together my approaches to the physicality of the book, learned from its beginnings as small press activity, through the various stages of it becoming more evident in the world. Hopefully, there is at the same time, a reductive learned from those earlier editorial principles that can be applied to all products of the imagination, especially the plastic arts.

It is an assembly of texts and pieces written over the last forty or more years for a variety of reasons and in many contexts. In grouping and collecting them together, an attempt is being made to assert and examine the possible model of the small publishing press as a way of working. Perhaps at first more literary in its ancestry, the small publishing press could be seen as the more durable foundation of the recent interest in books by artists and the whole idea of publication as a prime means of making. This, for me, has been the enduring platform of a means of making books and developing other materials for the physicality of the poem. This book could be seen as a companion to an earlier collection of commentary, *Some Forms of Availability: Critical Passages on the Book and Publication* (RGAP, 2007).

The texts here may be seen as appendices to the premise of one small publishing case-history deeply rooted in its attempt to find a model for its activities. The platform and exegesis of Coracle Press, and before it, Tarasque Press, was dealt with in more detail in *Some Forms of Availability*. These can be seen as directives in the development of a small press concerned critically with the implications of publishing. At the same time, they may point to wider developments arising from it, the editing of more physical spaces as extensions, organisationally and economically, of what begins with the book.

Hopefully, this will show that the small press platform can extend by example into other ways of working, through the application of its spirit of self-invention and economy of means: the primacy of its editorial reduction. Its final form may be not only the book and allied publications, but a unified approach to diverse fields of subjects and objects emanating from a common aesthetic. It is thereby a synthesis of attitudes, developed in the context of the aesthetics and economics of the small press, applied to wider concerns of approach to the making of things.

The artists' book, with its current prominence yet belated history and diverse methodology, cannot account for the true variety in the field of play of new books and the platform of publishing what could be called 'primary' books, in their own unclassifiable way. The dissolution of gallery presentation into printing and distribution as a way of working might be one route to the artists' book, but I have preferred referring to them as 'primary books', often by way of their inexplicability in terms of a genre, and the singularity of their means of classification in a new idiomatic field. Indeed the genre of the so-called artists' book may be best defined as classifying its one subject exhaustively.

But there is a pattern of the small literary press, and the models for it, that probably begins with the broadsheet, the single printed sheet, alongside various more ephemeral forms: the postcard, the extended invitation to an event, the poster, the larger print. The pattern progresses to an anthology of parts by various contributors, edited together to form a magazine, often referred to as 'the little magazine', and eventually this may lead to the pamphlet or chapbook, and ultimately the complete, individual book. Each of these formats has its own life in duration and sustainability.

There is sometimes an immediacy to the possibility of publishing and publication that exists in no other field, and I was recently thinking of the painter Ian Gardner who might in his earlier years draw round a piece of toast from his breakfast on a card and send it to a range of friends as a postcard, with an added text and date and time of writing. Later in life, and in his usual quizzical way, with serious disability, he begin his series 'At A Stroke' made and circulated in difficult circumstances. There is something about the genre that invites the confusion and contradiction of its separate parts, and as an example I remember fondly the postcard-magazine *Fishpaste* published by Rigby Graham in Leicester in the early 1960s, where he would invite an artist to illustrate a poem-text on the reverse side of a standard printed postcard with stamp placement position indicated.

Indeed, it is the pamphlet, political and discursive in its beginnings in the nineteenth century, which is now liberated to fulfil its new function as the means of the small publishing press. Maybe it is the political pamphlet of the time that becomes the adopted vehicle, rather than the rarefication of the private press, and certainly there is marked contrast between English and American developments, rooted in the ephemeral, and the more rarefied French tradition of the belle-livre.

From these beginnings, it may lead to the more full and accomplished book, tools developed, processes defined, as the knowledge of where to find things like paper and print increases. There is no longer any pejoratively 'small' or 'little', but there may be examples of forms and series of publications that can only exist within an alternative to commercial publishing. Indeed, the whole scope of this territory is the critical alternative of small press publishing.

Implied throughout is a consideration of the economic basis of production, of ways of working and survival that are endemic in The Small Press as a model of self-organisation. There is a completion and self-resolve in this mode of activity, where you can begin and operate as a way of living, in spite of the overbearing established conditions that surround us. It is a base, a reassessment of our need and priorities as producers for a working form, a fulfilment to begin something that can flourish.

And as such, it will probably relate to a community of similarly positioned activity, small publishing presses who are struggling to find a way, not competitively, but collaboratively and collectively, the true base of modernist work, a network.

Those first steps are probably domestic, working from the kitchen table, the cupboard under the stairs, stock held in cardboard boxes, stored as the beginnings of a warehouse. This accumulation of the 'titles' of your press, the backlist, is the ultimate stage of building its platform, the body of work to be chosen from, and that represents both its unity and divergence. This is often at odds with the medium of the artists' book which seems to predicate itself on the individuality of the single book and its physical manipulations, to be contrasted with the focus on 'content' of the small press publication.

This may arise from the way in which the editorial process involves and indicates production, the idea of the edition itself being part of the content of the publication. This is the exact opposite of the non-editorial process of 'print-on-demand' and its form of 'cassette' production, where the process has little bearing on the editorial form of the publication and its economic and community solutions.

The context of the new 'title' that you are making is in the unit of both the work itself, and also its overall presence, in the inherent multiple copies of its edition. These are the materials of that unit, its medium, to be distributed and spread out between readers. It is the whole of that 'title', in a discrete list of publications, that is the true work of this medium of the book. It is multiple in nature but singular in intention.

Indeed, sometimes the content of the book may almost be the paper itself, the materials, the divisibility of a sheet-size into a convenient page for the process of print and assembly. This intimately becomes part of the editorial process of reduction and realisation. As you will see further on, I began to identify a continuous series of books of my own as 'The Metaphor Books', whereby the physical nature of the book itself and its materials and material structure become the physical metaphor of the poem taking place.

The very diversity of the small press publication, its fragility, leads directly to its problematic presence in bookshops and libraries. The bookshop should be a clear extension of its platform allowing an unsuspecting audience to discover what it didn't know and which can only be assimilated by the synaesthesia of true browsing. Libraries are a longer-term matter and depend on the accumulation of the backlist of publications described earlier.

However, the dissemination of your publications will demand visits to book-buyers in various bookstores, your work as a travelling salesman. Libraries and appointments with librarians are a slower matter, but the placement of titles and the knowledge of the whereabouts of most copies of an edition are its essential.

Most of my time now is spent dealing with libraries and eclectic librarians, putting together assemblies from the backlist that might fit their collection, suggesting extensions of concern. This is really the function of the backlist and its variousness, and makes for units of financial return much more useful economically than the slow drip of single copies in more 'trade' conditions. Of course, you need both ways of distribution, and each copy of a book acquired is a reward of purpose. William Morris took great care in this form of hand-distribution, and I believe had printed in the colophon of later editions of the Kelmscott Press: "Sold by William Morris".

Eventually, you can work out what might be appropriate from your backlist to a given library holding, and spend much of your distribution time tailoring such lists. At the same time you must be open to the most obscure circumstances in which books can be produced and placed, and that have no precedent.

In certain circumstances, it may be that you have the space to work on only one book at a time, to make a title in a single place, an itinerant kind of publishing—to prepare, produce and distribute one book, and move on to a different address. It reminds me of Dick Higgins at Something Else Press in New York and New York State in the nineteen sixties and seventies, where he said that he might spend nine months in the planning and production of a given book, and then nine months on distribution. He would then consider the book finished, and nothing more could be done with it. (This probably accounts for why there were so many copies of certain SEP titles available as remainders at a given time!)

There have been times in the recent past when the very organisation of other physical spaces could be seen as a form of publishing, not merely for the surfaces and pages of printed material, but the making available of installed work as a series or format of presentation. For us at Coracle, this led to the examination of the rooms and spaces in Camberwell as formats in themselves, spaces equivalent to the publications. These were book spaces and that of the small gallery, and the improvisational nature of the small gallery could be learned from anthologising as small press activity, transferring that editorial playfulness to those more physical spaces.

Coracle was particularly influenced by an encounter in the late nineteen sixties with Brian Lane, who published several books of mine at that time. Earlier in the decade, he had run Gallery Number Ten, a small gallery and display space of a kind similar to Coracle, in a shop in Blackheath, where he exhibited the work of Ben Vautier, Jochen Gerz, Jiří Valoch, Timm Ulrichs, aspects of contemporary music and various unknown others. It was influential for me, despite resenting some of the work when I first came across it at that point in the 'sixties. But eventually resolving what Brian had actually done with his space and publishing, I began to see it as quite seminal. It sat outside the literary world in a certain way, and at the same time, it was outside the gallery and visual arts. Yet it brought more information to them. It was not blinkered by its own existence. It was always looking elsewhere. You could actually spend a lot of time discovering things there. The act of discovery was very important to it. It was not all one single space, where everything was revealed immediately. You had to read through it. So I think this idea of the format of the gallery also interacted with the ideas that arose for formats for books and the need for publications and invitation cards and catalogues that we made for shows at the gallery.

Eventually this led to the notion of physical spaces as a form of publishing for Coracle. The proposed Allotment series to be held in Liverpool in the late nineteen eighties only ran to the first 'issue', of Richard Long's *Stone Field*, owing to the immensity of scale of the project and the organisational politics of the occasion. There were many other 'titles' planned, and the whole format of Allotment allowed for the simultaneous presence of individual works running alongside each other, as in the eponymous title of the project. The whole project was conceived as an anthology of parts in what could be seen as a magazine. For us at Coracle, the Allotment project in Liverpool in the nineteen eighties was a kind of summation.

The whole synthesis can become a unit, an extension of publication itself. As you will see gathered in this book, the Coracle use of bookspaces was a means of encounter, of initial reading and discovery, well beyond the commerce of exchange. But perhaps the most developed critical spaces as forms of their own have been these bookspace interventions of Coracle over the last forty years. They are listed at the end of the first section of this book, under Locations. In the earlier days, book workshops were also held in various locations, official and unofficial situations and institutions. Unlike the bookspaces, these were not seen in any formatted way as an alternative model of publication, but just as a response to an educational and informational demand.

However, this duality of display and publishing has not always been without problems, and there have been times when it was necessary to go back to the table, to re-assess where the heightened visual was leading:

> To seek to rediscover a space and duration absent from much current gallery work. To propose a redemptive function for the exhibition, not a theme show but an activity. A process, not a catalogue, but an index of possibilities in a theoretical area to be defined.
>
> The work has no pejorative physical scale, and if it seeks to be monumental, it does so by other means. It is the opposite of sculpture and can work in the library as well as the gallery. The book may be its ideal form. It is a reference work and also a co-ordinating office for previous projects and others to be conducted. The installation respects the individual work in order to subvert it.
> —Card issued from Galleria Victoria Miro, Firenze, 1990.

As with *Some Forms of Availability*, this book is a gathering and collecting together of shorter items, reviews, etc., that already have been used in their initial context. It is however envisaged that they might come together in an anthological way to form a more central, syndromatic work.

Allotment, Liverpool—stills from the film of the project made by Colette Culbert between March and May 1987, available on YouTube: 'Richard Long Stone Field'.

"Light from the gantry in the roof of Renshaw Hall, eclipses the burning of the old dance floor, the maze of partitions and counters already removed from its time as the unemployment office. From the narrow entrance on Renshaw Street in the very centre of the city, through its dark passage, you arrive in the huge interior… The demolition gang worked for many weeks to clear the building. New shutters were fitted, large enough for lorries to enter from the Benson Street end."—*Control Magazine*, no.14: 'Art Creating Society', 1990.

Its first section, 'The Small Press Model', begins with texts that relate in the widest sense to the literary beginnings of two small publishing presses, from their formation, their developing activities, critical sides and hypotheses about what they make, moving towards more plastic concerns: the physicality of the book, its materials. At this point 'The Small Press Model' avoids the issue of the artists' book, preferring a more continuous development from literary ideas in the tradition of publishing that links it with the developments of modernism and collaboration in collective work.

'Equivalent Spaces' in turn goes beyond the book and published work to itemise occasions of confusion and uncertainty of category. These may have developed from the initial concerns of the possibilities of publishing, but have moved on from more domestic arrangements, to the gallery exhibition and objects, as with the previous section, informed by the stance and sensibility of making things available, to be discovered, looked at and handled. Even when a text seems to deal almost exclusively with exhibitions and purely visual phenomena, it is hoped that the aesthetic platform was informed from the beginning by the model and intentions of small press activity.

'Equivalent Spaces' also harbours the idealised notion that physical space might be equivalenced by a printed version of itself, the capacity of a sequence of printed and folded pages to be parallel to a room or installation in the more physical world, a key to understanding and bringing it to scale, a kind of architecture of the book.

In 'Particular Dislocations', the book begins to encroach even further on the world of galleries and places of presentation, and many of the entries here may be merely responses to specific situations and occasions in a critical manner.

For all this generic activity, it is a fulfilment of one of the precepts of modernism in which I believe implicitly: the collective, collaborative work. But in these times of lockdown from pandemic disease, and since, most things have faltered in their continuity. A bigger threat to the physical dexterity of the book, more significant than digitalisation by a long way, is the productional slowness of things, the constant re-assessment of what is left. This, attached to the decline of always proverbial market economics, amounts to an almost impossible place to begin.

Finally, however, I must return to a near-romantic belief in the poem itself, not only as subject, but as the endurance of its fragility beyond physical bounds, its persistence, endeavour, the heroism and hedonism of its continuation. Lives built and lived to support it. How lyric can be sustained into old age.

The Small Press Model

'Collective Work in the Critical Mode' is adapted from an essay written for inclusion in *Code-X: Paper, Ink, Pixel and Screen*, bookRoom, 2015; also published in 'BLAST at 100: A Modernist Magazine Reconsidered', edited by Philip Coleman, Kathryn Milligan, and Nathan O'Donnell, *Literary Modernism*, Vol.3, Brill, 2017.

'Ian Hamilton Finlay's Wild Hawthorn Press' was published in *Ceolfrith* 5: 'Ian Hamilton Finlay', Sunderland: Bookshop Gallery, 1970.

'The South Bank Show' is from the boxed catalogue to the "festival of work made in the South of London", which was held at the following venues: Coracle Press, South London Art Gallery, Sally East Gallery, and Morley Gallery, 16th April–20th May 1982.

'The Metaphor Books' is adapted from the transcript of an illustrated talk given at Granary Books, New York, 21st July 2009.

'Notes on The Unpainted Landscape' the foreword and introduction to *The Unpainted Landscape*, the accompanying publication to a Scottish Arts Council group exhibition which toured to six venues during 1987.

'Allotment', parts published previously in *The Coracle: Coracle Press Gallery 1975-1987*, Yale Centre for British Art, 1989; and *Uniformagazine*, no.4, Autumn 2015.

'The Presence of Landscape', from the catalogue *The Presence of Landscape: Printed Objects, Cards & Books, Coracle Press 1975-2000* at Centre Culturel Jean Gagnant, Limoges, 14th March–7th April 2000.

'The Vinyl Project', introduction to the book which accompanied the exhibition *Vinyl: Project for installation*, at the Christian Brothers School, Cork, July and August 2005.

'Certain Trees' is an adapted version of the introduction and artists' summaries in the book which accompanied the exhibition *Certain Trees: The Constructed Book, Poem and Object 1967-2006*; Centre des Livres d'Artistes, Saint-Yrieix-la-Perche, France, 10th June–16th September 2006; the Library at the Van Abbemuseum, Eindhoven, Netherlands, 11th November 2007–4th January 2008; and the Victoria and Albert Museum, South Kensington, London SW7, late February–August 2008.

'The Norfolk Years' was published as the introduction to *Printed in Norfolk: Coracle Publications 1989–2012*, RGAP, 2012; which accompanied the exhibition at Norwich University College of the Arts, 20th March–21st April; Shandy Hall, Coxwold, 15th September–14th October; Saison Poetry Library, Royal Festival Hall, London, 1st–30th November 2012.

'Construction Storage Despatch', is adapted from the introduction to the book of this title about the work of Martin Rogers, Coracle, 2015.

'Made in English' is adapted from the postscript to *Made in English: The Poems of Stuart Mills*, Coracle, 2008.

'Threads in Relationship to Kettle's Yard', 'At Last', and 'Living and Publishing in Tipperary' are previously unpublished.

Collective Work in the Critical Mode

It could be that the Little Magazine as we know it began with the Pre-Raphaelite Brotherhood's *The Germ*. Never before had there been a common critical platform that combined visual art, poetry and literature on a collective aesthetic basis. It was the genesis of the collective work of Modernism, and the beginnings of a common work of collaboration, well beyond the Renaissance assertion of the attic genius.

This was taken up by the Vorticists and *BLAST*, and for a short period of time asserted the equanimity of artists and poets within a common aesthetic. The manifesto-like qualities of *BLAST* will always have a wryness for the English sensibility, which does not detract from an idealised unity of purpose of its collective whole. It was this tone of ironic declaration and muted proclamation that we responded to at Tarasque Press, beginning in the mid-nineteen sixties.

Stuart Mills had the idea for *Tarasque* magazine and a small publishing press of the same name when he began the Trent Bookshop in Nottingham in 1964. I joined him shortly afterwards and we began production. It was an innocent enough adventure, and the legend of the Tarasque monster arising from the River Rhône to ravage the surrounding countryside had critical potency. From then on, our readings took us to the beginnings of English Modernism, to Pound, Lewis and the Vorticists, and the tone of *BLAST* as a pivotal little magazine, and we thought we might adopt some of it.

Later we were joined by Ian Gardner, screen-printer and minimal panel-maker, providing us with more physical possibilities than the treadle-platen letterpress machine we were trying to master. From the flatness of colour of screen-printing, he later took up watercolour painting in a most elemental way, and his reductionist approach fitted our formative aesthetic. Collaborative efforts were often aimed towards some sort of quasi-manifesto-like stance, not without the humour of parody. Ian Hamilton Finlay had begun to join in too, with contributions to the magazine, the seminal *Ocean Stripe 5*, and the screen prints of *Acrobats* and *Star/Steer*. We began to develop what came to be called the critical mode of Tarasque, which stayed with us all collaboratively and individually. In this we proposed that an imaginative, primary work could be made of and from criticism, and we inferred this from Lewis and *BLAST*, the Vorticists in general, and the Pound of 'Hugh Selwyn Mauberley'.

Stuart Mills went on to publish his monographic magazine *Aggie Weston's*, named after the small homes for seamen, and with its

Tarasque, nos.1–11 & 12, Nottingham, 1965 to 1971. "Tarasque: An animal which lived on the banks of the Rhône in France and ravaged the surrounding countryside until it was overcome."

allusion to a collage of Kurt Schwitters. Ian Gardner briefly issued his proto-manifesto sheet *The Blue Tunnel*, much in the manner of Tarasque's *Private Tutor*. I began and developed Coracle as a way of publishing in an even more material form by means of physical space.

Stuart Mills had already paid his respects to Wyndham Lewis with his postcard: "wordswords/wordswords/wordswords/wordswords/wordswords", and we began to cite even more fully the influence of that previous era upon us, in the ultimate issue of *Tarasque* magazine, Nos.11 & 12:

> *Tarasque* is edited by Stuart Mills and Simon Cutts from the Trent Book Shop, Trent Bridge, Nottingham.
> Back issues of the magazine are available, all except No.1. which is now out of print. Poets whose work has been included or discussed in past issues include Peter Armstrong; Stephen Bann; Pete Brown; Basil Bunting; Simon Cutts; Ronald Duncan; Ian Hamilton Finlay; Roy Fisher; Robert Garioch; Ray Gosling; Hugh

Creighton Hill; George Hitchcock; Anselm Hollo; Libby Houston; David McAndrew; Stuart Mills; Stephen Scobie; Charles Tomlinson; Gael Turnbull.

This double issue marks the end of the present series. Although running over into the 70s *Tarasque* has really been a magazine of the 60s; a dissenting voice, out of tune with most little presses. The function of the little magazine will remain fundamentally the same even though that cloud of dust thrown up by the stampede of carpetbaggers during the last decade has obscured this function. It is to grasp the significance of certain shifts away from the commonplace at a given period. It is to remain firmly not a part of any broad based movement but to pluck from such movements figures who perhaps themselves out of context miss the relevance of their own achievement, and it is to be supremely arrogant.

Anyone who has studied a representative selection of small magazines from the so called 'British Underground' during the last ten years will have noted a general aimlessness. The same names appear again and again, and with one or two rare exceptions, the covers like the contents seem interchangeable. In a recent issue of *Agenda* William Cookson makes the following comment:

> I believe that Lewis' writing and painting is particularly pertinent to the state of the arts at the beginning of the 70s so this issue is not intended to be purely retrospective. The extremism, the nullity and the blight of fashion—emotion without intellect, fancy without imagination—which Lewis attacked throughout his life are everywhere prevalent, not only in sculpture and painting but in poetry.

A whole generation has been hoodwinked by the prophets of the new, and it will take perhaps another generation for the damage to be undone. We are not, as Michael Horovitz would have us believe, on the verge of a new age. Poetry will not be resuscitated by troupes of performing mountebanks, and it is a fierce thought that for some time to come his anthology *Children of Albion* will be the most comprehensive selection of poetry from the 60s.

We spared little. It was in the first round-up of Tarasque production and associate workings, entitled *Metaphor and Motif*, that Stephen Bann first coined the term "critical mode" to describe some of our activities, and it still seems redolent and relevant. The cover of this travelling display and its poster was Ian Gardner's *Bath Mat: A Constructivist Flag*, firstly done as a watercolour and then a screenprint (overleaf), and finally reproduced in black and white.

Ian Gardner, *Bath Mat: A Constructivist Flag*, 1972.

The Critical Mode developed into more of a Questioning Mode, where the interrogation became part of the collective spirit of the occasion. Hence, the *Private Tutor* series was begun in 1967 and ran to the end of the decade.

No.8 in the series was Ian Hamilton Finlay's poem 'Arcady', where after the rendition of the poem itself, the footnotes become a series of questions on its general nature, but nonetheless part of its form:

Arcady
ABCDEFGHIJKLMNOPQRSTUVWXYZ

Some Questions on the Poem
1. The poem is no more than an alphabet with a title. Why should an alphabet be presented as a poem and given the title 'Arcady'?
2. 'Roam' is a verb we associate with 'Arcady', Can one roam among the letters of the alphabet? Might it be that the letters can be compared to the fields and forests, mosses and springs of an ancient pastoral landscape? If so, why?
3. Is it relevant to other effects of the poem that the letters are given caps, when they might be in lower case? Could letters possibly have existed before words? Can you imagine their appearance?
4. The original Dada-ists of 1916 wrote a number of poems composed entirely of single letters. Do you think that 'Arcady' is, a) a non-poem; b) a new-Dada poem; c) a poem that tries to civilise a neo-Dada cliche by turning it into a light-hearted classical conceit?

A Question on the Questions
In your opinion do the questions show a classical conceit?

PRIVATE TUTOR August 1967   issue No.1.

Assuming from the onset that the reader has little or no grounding in literature we will commence and continue in a very direct manner.

TO THE YOUNG WOULD-BE POET, FIRST SOME WARNINGS.

NEVER   Trust the heart
AVOID   Whenever possible the photographs of other poets even though you may admire them.
NEVER   Expect to discover a fruitful relationship with more than three other poets.
Never   Try to make people ashamed of themselves
Never   Try to make people respect you
Never   Try to appear harmless and good
Never   Try to influence politicians
Never   Try to define poetry.

FIRST EXERCISE.

    Obtain a copy of John Millington Synge's poetry.
    Read all the poems.
    Decide which one you prefer.
    For the next month show only this poem to your acquaintances, send only this poem to all the editors you intend to inundate, always explaining carefully why you like it.
    Write no poetry during this month.

Should you find nothing of interest in Synge you will obviously be unable to commit yourself to one of the poems. Instead, answer _briefly_ the following questions;

1. Why do you think Synge wrote so little.
2. Does Synge's interest in Villon signify anything.
3. Might one reasonably assume Synge to be more a dabbler than a real poet.
4. Indicate the general themes in Synge's poetry.
5. How do these differ from your own intentions.

Tarasque Press   The Trent Book Shop   Trent Bridge   Nottingham

Private Tutor Issue No.1, August 1967, Tarasque Press.

"*Private Tutor* arose out of the whole critical spirit of Tarasque, the press and magazine, and its early issues included many highly critical pieces opposing the grain of the times, the late-sixties. Audience was never a big issue, and it really was for a small circuit of poets and writers who were in close contact (Ian Hamilton Finlay had the idea that you made work for about six people finally), although libraries and other individuals had a subscription. A couple of hundred copies were printed of each one: given the means of production, you made the publication and suffered the consequences afterwards.

After Finlay's *P.O.T.H.*, it seemed that a magazine could be very slight, even just a sheet of polemics like *Private Tutor*. It surfaced as a burlesque, a caprice on the mood of the magazine. The 'L' was for the plates on the cars of learner drivers. Its humour was in its faux didacticism, and the notion that a lot of poets out there needed to get educated more."
—From a written interview with Marie Boivent, University of Rennes, 2011

A few years later, the form was taken up briefly, in *The Blue Tunnel*, by Ian Gardner who was working by then in the north of England, as a founder of the New Arcadians group of artists, critics and writers. One issue heralded a view of the particular plasticity of the artists and writers of Nottingham, influenced by small scale models and other functional objects as a concentration of motifs for work:

> "nor has the acridity
> of tobacco
> replaced the savouriness
> of food"
> —Guillaume Apollinaire 'Les Peintres Cubistes'
>
> nor the horrors
> of war
> diminished the plasticity
> of the tank

One of the persistent motifs was in fact the abstraction of the weather, and Stuart Mills quoted Ian Hamilton Finlay in his introduction: "The proper subjects for poetry are: the Seasons, the Affections, Fishing Boats, Inland Waterways, Non-Alcoholic Beverages, Certain Flowers, Certain Trees. Improper subjects are: Sex, Drugs, War and Self. Adjectives should be used sparsely, if at all, and not ever in proportion of more than one to every 9 nouns."

Tarasque 10 summer number

Its focus gave rise to the summer issue of *Tarasque*, No.10, (above) with a continuation of the theme, suggested by the presence of the Newark weed-boat on the River Trent in North Nottinghamshire. In response, Ian Hamilton Finlay provided *The Weed Boat Masters Ticket Part 1*, where the full extent of the critical and interrogational mode became a new prime work in its own right:

> Q.3. Study the following inventory. Pick out three items to give you the impression of a steam-powered herring drifter, INS 1.
>
> Coal-scuttle, herring-net, anchor, teapot, thimble, funnel, porthole, tea-caddy, coal-shovel, crystal-set, galley-stove, fishing-numerals, steam-pipe, fish-basket, flag.

Ian Gardner had produced a small assembly called *Allotments*, a collaboration between himself, Ian Hamilton Finlay, Stuart Mills and me, the writings of the latter two reflecting the preoccupation with further objects of weather. The tone was even more of ironic manifesto:

> Felt by itself is not a hat
> yet this blue ribbon
> is a flag,
> the winds cravat.
>
> .
>
> To the initiated they bring almost instant meaning.
> It is doubtful whether flags will ever become
> obsolete no matter what advances science may offer.

But the fullest occasion of this preoccupation may have been the Coracle group exhibition *The Weather House and other works*, in Nottingham in 1975 (overleaf), the catalogue and critical polemic of its introduction:

> I still work with the notion to hand that the group phenomenon is the most important characteristic of the modern movement, in its pursuit of aesthetic centre. It still remains the only valid approach to a working position independent of the barriers that separate 'the arts'. It is a discovery of the "glue" that makes a painting cohere with a poem, a construction with even a piece of music. This may be too emphatic, to endorse too heavily a natural projection arising between artists who simply have something in common.

In 1974 Martin Fidler and me had silkscreened *The Allies* on a kitchen table. It improvised on the notion of war games and the objects involved, its elaborate sewing and cutting a kind of constructivist camouflage for the cover of the book. Response to *The Allies* was rapidly returned in the new genre by a collaboration from Ian Hamilton Finlay and his son (shown p.27).

Martin Fidler & Simon Cutts, *The Allies*, 1974

The Weather House and other works: Coracle Press Exhibition, Midland Group Gallery, 1975.

"Anthology for the pages of this catalogue and for the walls and spaces of the Midland Group Gallery" Nottingham, 5–26 July 1975. Work by Simon Cutts, Karl Torok, Martin Fidler, Stephen Skidmore, David Willetts, Ian Gardner, Stephen Duncalf, Kay Roberts, Stuart Mills; catalogue texts by Stephen Bann, Simon Cutts (below), Edward Lucie-Smith.

>'Stephen Skidmore: a posthumourous note'
>
>He was carrying his watercolourists' suitcase, the one-time guard or train driver from the narrow gauge railway. It was a time of prolonged disappearance into the cafes and guest houses of Inverness where he had a bread round and was losing money on the cream buns.
>
>He speculated on the next move, a kind of throw of the coin between Carlisle or Sheffield. Much of the conversation hovered on whether or not you should leave the pencil lines in a watercolour; whether Paul Nash did it or not.
>
>He had arrived on the night train for a curry.

 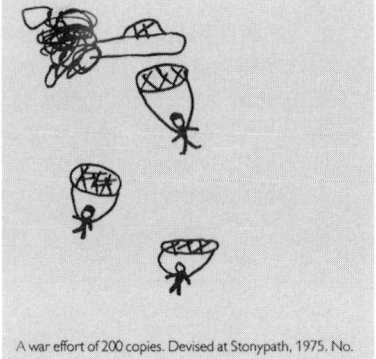

Ian Hamilton Finlay & Alexander Finlay, *The Axis*, Wild Hawthorn Press, 1975.

Stuart Mills continued collaborations with the loose assembly of artists and writers, and the 1979 book, *Professor Thomas Bodkin and Cezanne*, takes potentially ironic texts from the renowned art historian, and sets them alongside drawings by Stephen Duncalf. Again, the critical context of a subject is used to make it a primary work:

> The contours
> of even the simplest objects
> still continue to elude him
> .
>
> He seldom succeeds in placing
> a reflection at the correct angle
> to the thing reflected
> .
>
> Cezanne often makes a tree trunk
> grow thicker as it ascends
> .
>
> But it may be fairly said of him
> that if he stumbles often
> in his road home it is because
> he is hampered by his wings

Over the years I have used a continued critique of the work of the artist Andy Goldsworthy as a work in itself in the critical mode, as in the *A. Goldsworthy Questionnaires* of 1996:

> As a topic of my thesis I have chosen *snow* and i would like to include you in it. I have enclosed a short questionnaire for each subject, and if you could find time to fill in some of the questions, I would be extremely grateful.

Q
1. What is your earliest memory of *snow*
2. When and how did you first use the concept of *snow*
3. Is *snow* a constant theme in your work
4. What properties do you find unique to *snow*
5. What advantages do you find in working with *snow*
6. What disadvantages do you find when using *snow*

A
1. ....
2. ....
3. ....
4. ....
5. ....
6. ....

These have been followed by a gathering of all their parts in 'The A. Goldsworthy Productions' of 2012, alongside versions of miniprinter poems, a form of five lines of thirty characters and spaces:

Have you heard of an artist
called Andy Goldsworthy?
Her Grace wanted him to make
something up on the Moor
with loose sheep droppings.

The cover and sub-text of Stuart Mills' collected poems, published as *Made in English* in 2006, reinforces the kind of lineage we tried to make collectively through our critical mode, at once concrete, found, mis-heard, and critically positioned as near-manifesto.

Made in English / Iron in Wetness / Washing Will

Ian Hamilton Finlay's Wild Hawthorn Press

By the sixties the little press scene had largely become an ethic of duplicated sheets, smudges and absence of layout—a harbinger of the 'underground'. The possibility of inexpensive circulation made dizzy literally hundreds of new editors exchanging sofas for Gestetners in their living-rooms. Unlike their forerunners in the earlier part of the century, most of the new little presses sought to abandon scrutiny and discernment and foster a completely unconscious brand of expressiveness to attract what remained of an unrecruited audience. There were—and are—of course, noble exceptions to this general pattern. For these exceptions the only real distinction a small press might have from a commercial publisher should be that it chooses to publish seemingly unsaleable goods in small editions, and that this difference in role should not lower the quality of production.

Wild Hawthorn Press in not only an exception in the general dreary scene just mentioned, but is also an exception to all categories of publishing classification. With a range of work and standard of production equalling and often surpassing those to be found in any kind of publishing, it is a singular achievement.

Ian Hamilton Finlay wanted to do two things. Firstly, make available the work of good poets whose work demanded but was not receiving presentation, and, secondly, to provide a platform for his own work.

It was a case of wanting the best and producing it himself: for the sake of quality and not just quickness, Wild Hawthorn Press has published Finlay's own work largely because he does not feel that any other publisher or press could do it successfully.

An outstanding achievement is the magazine *Poor.Old.Tired.Horse.*, publication of which is now temporarily suspended but which ran to twenty-five issues almost as regularly as any commercial publication. One must compare what Finlay produced for 9d (plus postage and packaging 3d) with what the little press editor at large would consider the price of his stencil. He managed to do this by applying inexpensive printing techniques to seemingly elaborate illustrations and layout, often combining hand written poems and illustrations printed by cheap offset. The achievement is also due to the wide-ranging collaboration with designers and artists not usually thought of as being within the scope of a little press. Finlay has maintained this width of collaboration not only in his own work for this medium of print but also in solid and three-dimensional work.

The scope of *P.O.T.H.* was formidable. It is difficult enough to think of any other poetry sheet so simple and yet delightful, let alone consider that it brought together such names as Ad Reinhardt, Earl Haig, Charles Biederman, Pierre Albert-Birot, Theodore Enslin and Bridget Riley. Also, before production was suspended numbers embodying work by Vasarely and Mathias Goeritz had been planned. This bringing together is even more delightful when one considers that the poems were presented in issues going under such headings as 'Lollipop Number' (No.11) and 'Teapoth' (No. 23). Poems used have often been rescued from oblivion: who besides Finlay cared to remember, for instance, Hamish Maclaren after 1929, whose poem 'Little Sea House' was used in *P.O.T.H.* 15 (Boats. Shores. Tides. Fish. Anthology issue.)

> Little sea house
>   When I found you,
> The yellow poppies
>   Were nodding round you.
>
> Your blue slate hat
>   That the four winds
> Came to tug at
>   Over the tamarinds:
>
> I remember it well:
>   The salmon nets drying—
> Laugh, violin-shell,
>   And cease crying:
>
> For I will return
>   Through the sea haze:
> I am sailing back there
>   Always, always.

P.O.T.H. had far more variety and range than the combination of Ian Hamilton Finlay and concrete poetry might suggest. This variety ties in with Finlay's aesthetic of all art, which is something beyond and before the compulsive modernism of the avant-garde often propagated by the small press.

The list of books produced by Wild Hawthorn Press runs from Erik Satie to Jonathan Williams, and includes Lorine Niedecker, Robert Lax, Augusto de Campos as well as Finlay's own magnanimous collaborations with many designers, illustrators and typographers.

Perhaps the press's greatest contribution to publication has been the poem/print, corresponding more to book publication in the large number of the edition, rather than to prints from fine art publishers. This particular contribution has not as yet been truly credited to Finlay, and Christopher Logue seems to receive continued notice for its development, although he did not use his first poem/print until 1965, whereas Finlay's series began in 1963. This mode of publication is a logical development of the concrete presentation of a poem, and it is interesting to note that Wild Hawthorn has produced the only consistently successful series of prints done over a period of years.

In the later sixties, because of the tightening concerns of its founder, the press has become the platform solely of Ian Hamilton Finlay himself, producing further prints, cards and books at an equal rate and with even more developed production than in the earlier more various list. And so, the tiny applecog gears of Wild Hawthorn Press have turned over to become his personal circulating point; as such, with a range almost equal to that of the generalised list, it continues.

The South Bank Show

Soon after beginning the bookspace and gallery at Coracle Press in 1976, we found that we needed to put ourselves on the map in both the physical and metaphysical dimension. Following an idea from Nicholas Logsdail of Lisson Gallery, Kay Roberts began the listing *New Exhibitions of Contemporary Art* in May 1978 from Coracle Press. Apart from filling a gap in the whole field of contemporary art in London which no-one seemed to have tackled earnestly until this point, its intentions were to direct attention to the galleries and studio activities on the edge of the known art map of London. The idea of *The South Bank Show* also came out of this situation.

Coracle Press, 233 Camberwell New Road, London SE5

Sally East, for example, had already begun to show and consolidate work of a most difficult kind at her gallery, firstly in New Church Road,

Camberwell, and later almost adjacent to Coracle Press in Camberwell New Road. After suggesting the idea of a *South Bank Show* to her, an approach was then made to Lesley Greene at the Greater London Arts Association, and at her suggestion, to Kenneth Sharpe at the South London Art Gallery. Its title was to be deliberately cribbed from London Weekend Television's meagre arts programme for its strength and directness when reapplied to our own situation.

Whilst it is still true that the visitors to Coracle Press Gallery are as likely to come from Reykjavik or Edinburgh as from Peckham, in a period between 1977 and 1980 by far the majority of the exhibitions at Coracle Press were made with artists known and unknown, who had walked through the door of the gallery unannounced, and who lived and worked locally. At the same time, the critical impasse from writers on art who live in the main only a mile or so away is as appalling as ever. An early awareness of the locality came through Tom Phillips' continuous project '20 Sites n Years' which was shown in full in the gallery in 1976. Each year Phillips photographs each of twenty different sites from the same marked spot or position on the map and from the same direction and inclination. The sites radiate from his home in Grove Road, Camberwell. When seen together, the evidence of change in the same site over a period of what is almost now ten years begins to tell its tale. There are aspects and implications

Tom Phillips, '20 Sites n Years': Peckham Road, 1973/82.

to this particular project which focus directly and humorously on the crass management of our immediate locale. In this case for both the artist and all his sites, and the publishing gallery, it happens to be the arena of the London Borough of Southwark, which is equally not notorious for its overwhelming support of the arts.

On that count, I can remember when Coracle Press had applied to have its rates reduced as an operation which may have added something to its surroundings. We were visited by a fairly large contingent from the Treasurer's Department. After being shown the gallery and some of the books made at Coracle Press, there was considerable discussion amongst themselves of a rather perplexed kind, and after some minutes a spokesman addressed me: "Well sir, we don't think we can help you in this case. If you were a scout hut, then we could."

There is, however in the locality and within the jurisdiction of the mentioned London Borough, the very wonderful building of the South London Art Gallery. I, for one, am convinced that it could be one of the finest spaces anywhere for showing work. It would take £10,000 to remove the hospital lighting and equivalence the almost full overhead lighting by concealment, and to surface the walls uniformly. One of the real purchases of the exhibition is to hang the South London Art Gallery as the focus of a large group exhibition of this kind. Its name is also polemic for the task.

Most of us labour cynically, some even defeatedly, with the knowledge that the tea-shoppes of Cork and Bond Streets do little to reflect the vitality and variety of work being produced, and at the same time the public arts organisations fail to find formats applicable to the problem. *The South Bank Show* was conceived as a festival of the width and quality of work produced between Rotherhithe and Wandsworth on the South Bank of the river. With the collaboration of Caryn Faure Walker as exhibition co-ordinator, we began to assemble a show for which there seemed very little precedent. Without a reasonable period in which to research the exhibition, we still had to arrive at a greater knowledge of what was around us than we already had. To do this we asked some fifty artists who constituted our initial list and who we thought might be attuned to the spirit of this show as a celebration, to bring our attention to three more artists each, making a total of one hundred and fifty. The final exhibition was then selected from the body of work of these artists, alongside the residual fifty.

Perhaps only the *British Painting 1974* exhibition at the Hayward Gallery had a parallel structure, but it remained clearly within the confines of a specific area of work. Some of the work coming into this exhibition has already given a great deal of pleasure, and we hope this can be shared. Now it remains to site very dissonant work together and believe that we can achieve a fusion of some sort. Amongst the work, I have noticed the current strength of a very literal statement, which has nothing whatsoever to do with the notion of 'figuration'.

The Coracle Press contribution to this exhibition may be its catalogue, whose format is culled from its own past group exhibitions of a thematic kind. For the *Miniatures 1977* exhibition we produced a

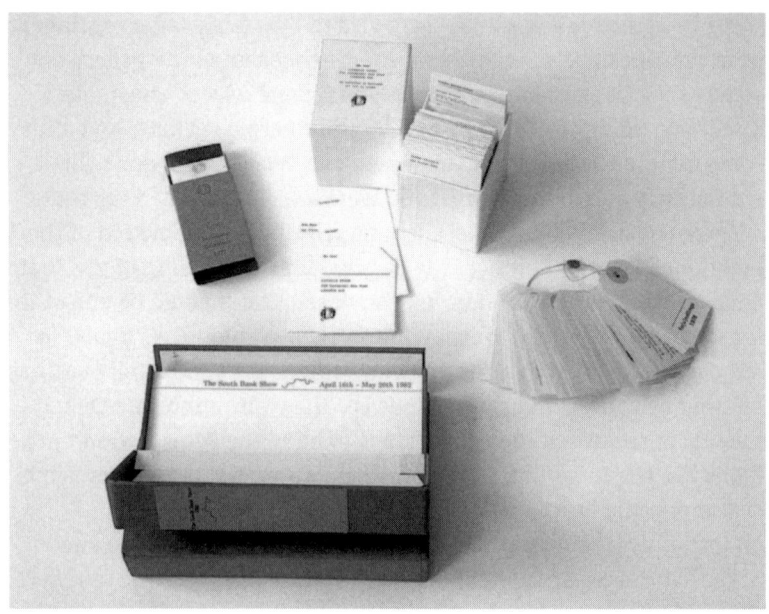

Coracle Press catalogues for group exhibitions. Top, left to right: *Miniatures*, 1977; *'On loan'*, 1980; *fo(u)ndlings*, 1978; below: *The South Bank Show*, 1982.

catalogue of cigarette cards inside a cigarette packet in order to carry the whole exhibition around in your pocket. For *fo(u)ndlings 1978* the catalogue was a boxed clump of tied labels, each one to be attached to a work inside the exhibition. The catalogue for the *On loan* exhibition in 1980 was the closest to date to this for *The South Bank Show*, and consisted of readers' tickets in book-pockets filed alphabetically as a small library index. Thus, this catalogue, hopefully reflecting the informational nature of the exhibition and at the same time endorsing some kind of loose-leaf system as the most adaptive format for open or group exhibitions (not to mention all that is possible to achieve within such limited timing).

Often where you come to start from in a city of this size is an arbitrary place. You begin to build with what is immediately to hand, and if the responses are not too hardened by survival, it may become particular. More often, however, you are there because it is cheap to make work which has little immediate outcome. As to more purposeful questions of an identity to the matter, there are few of us who can answer clearly.

Beyond such pragmatism, a tradition may begin to emerge, one which may have changed its location somewhat recently from the East End to the South of London. The enormous congregation of artists in this area is not reflected in any of the facilities available, and it has become the task of this exhibition to draw attention to it by its celebration.

London is also divided by attitudes to its physical geography that are indeed most curious. The reluctance of North Londoners to cross the river to the south, (or for that matter for South Londoners to cross the river to the north), has always been a source of amusement, amazement, and finally frustration. Imagine Paris divided by a river in any negative way!

As an American friend remarked: "If you live in a city, you should treat it like a city." Most Londoners don't seem to. Like them, I have come to think that all our problems happen and are solved in our own back yard, and that this city is really a succession of villages with no centre.

The Metaphor Books

I have prepared this talk in the light of last night's reading at St Mark's in the Bowery, where I was dealing with qualities of air and sound as a quotient in the poems I write. Today, I'm really talking about the physical form of some of the books and pamphlets, which may be going in a different direction. They may embody elements of air and sound in their text, but in their physical manifestation as objects is the thing I want to discuss now.

I started working in the early sixties in Nottingham, England, where I met the poet Stuart Mills. We began a press called Tarasque Press in the back of a bookshop called the Trent Bookshop. Stuart and his partner ran the bookshop, while Stuart and I ran Tarasque Press together, beginning with a magazine called Tarasque, which ran to twelve numbers.

During this time we began to feel very experimental and felt that we wanted to move away from just a small literary magazine and into more adventurous publications. We just worked by trial and error at what we were doing, but we had a sort of instinct that we really could do things with type and paper and how you divide them up. We bought a small platen printing press ourselves, which we were awkward with and could hardly handle at all. It took us years to actually begin to do things properly but there were trade printers in the town, very good letterpress printers, big industrial places, whom we could talk to and get to do things we needed.

I suddenly realised that I was interested in the transparency of sheets of paper and variable lines of coloured type. I did have some ideas for using the possibilities of the transparency of paper and one of the first things I did was *Claude Monet in his Water-Garden*. I'm not sure where this came from exactly—the poem, the idea of this poem itself—but in part it came from the idea of transparency. I was very involved in the whole idea of Impressionism: the notion that there might be some sort of theory of Impressionism. A theory, I guess, of what became more stylised as chaos theory later on. But at the time—the mid- to late sixties—it was really an idea that in Monet's paintings there were particular camouflages that were about the form of the piece. For instance, in the *Nympheas* painting, which is in the Orangerie in Paris, fault lines of false seams are painted into the round parts of the painting, so that a viewer gets used to the idea of seeing seams, or breaks in the installation of the canvases I was completely engaged in this scenario in the late nineteen sixties, and made a small book called *Camouflages*.

So *Claude Monet in his Water-Garden* was a succession of pages that could be read through, and it was really dealing with an image of Monet himself. I'd seen photographs of Monet in his garden at Giverny, thus "Claude Monet in his Water-Garden", "Claude Monet in his Floating Studio", "Claude Monet in his greenhouse".

That was really all the book was, just to see through the succession of transparent pages. Of course, there are always mistakes in the first things you make. I put two kinds of stanzaed poems in the back of the book which are completely unnecessary and they shouldn't be there.

This was a beginning with materials of printing at an edge—for me, an extreme edge, and being able to find the right kind of trade printers to be able to make something like that and begin to construct a poem which relied on the physical nature of the thing that was being produced. That facility quickly led to another work of almost transparent paper.

White Butterflies, 1968, was made by the same printer on manifold paper, another tissue-like paper. It is simply two permutations of a poem, and perhaps makes amends for leaving those two stanzas in the back of the previous book, because the two here are dialectically set against each other as almost the only offering of the book.

Haphazard camouflage	*Haphazard camouflage*
amongst butterflies:	*amongst cauliflowers:*
White cauliflowers	*White butterflies*

They're printed in yellow and there's a symmetry about the centre of the book, even the rusty staples, and it is compounded by the

Claude Monet in his Water-Garden, Tarasque Press, 1967.

physicality of the whole thing. Because the paper was so thin, it often rucked and blemished and made ripples when it was being saddle-stitched, stapled, and that's also part of it too, part of the decoration, the symmetry of the wings of the butterfly.

At this point I tried to print a book on almost transparent paper myself on the press that Stuart Mills and I had bought for Tarasque. It took one particular painting by Claude Monet entitled *Rue Montorgueil Decked Out with Flags*, a painting on the Fourth of July, decked out with flags for celebration, and you could see down the street at the accumulation of them. In a way, it became an emblematic picture for me. The text of the book reads as "sky / hyphen / patch"—with the hyphen being a coloured slug of orange, and the text fragments becoming "sky / hyphen", and eventually just "sky".

You turn the pages as if you were walking down the street. The pages in this book suggest that you could make this walk down rue Montorgueil with all the flags hanging above you, and back again, if you so wished.

At the same time as this, I made a glass version of this poem where the actual text was sand-blasted into the glass, and the indentations in-filled with colour, and I don't know what happened to that piece. Perhaps it was broken. A few years ago, a young book dealer in London asked to remake it in a small edition, so it does exist. We changed its nature to some extent. My first glass piece was just panels of glass held up in wooden bases. It was now made as a solid object, with the glass plates following each other in a box frame. It's a book-scale object, with a certain depth, by which the reflections of each plate of glass onto the next one create an even bigger sense of the organised chaos that I was suggesting existed in Impressionist thinking, and trying to take it a bit further. There are some issues of transparency that I tried to form around the book as an object that clearly do extend the metaphor of the poem.

In 1982, I made this small thing, almost nothing in a way, which was just a four-page pamphlet sewn with a single stitch, and on the cover is an image of the single knot inside, just blind-stamped on the cover (right, actual size). The title of this book is a knot pressed into the cover. And the only thing in the book says, "A fold of sewn cotton", and an ampersand "&", which is like the very knot itself. It is perhaps just a total affectation, celebrating the very action of making such things.

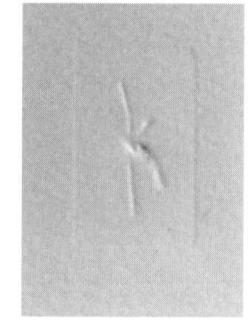

A fold of sewn cotton, Coracle Press, 1982.

38 THE SMALL PRESS MODEL

Rue Montorgueil Decked Out with Flags, sand-blasted and painted glass, 1971/2006.

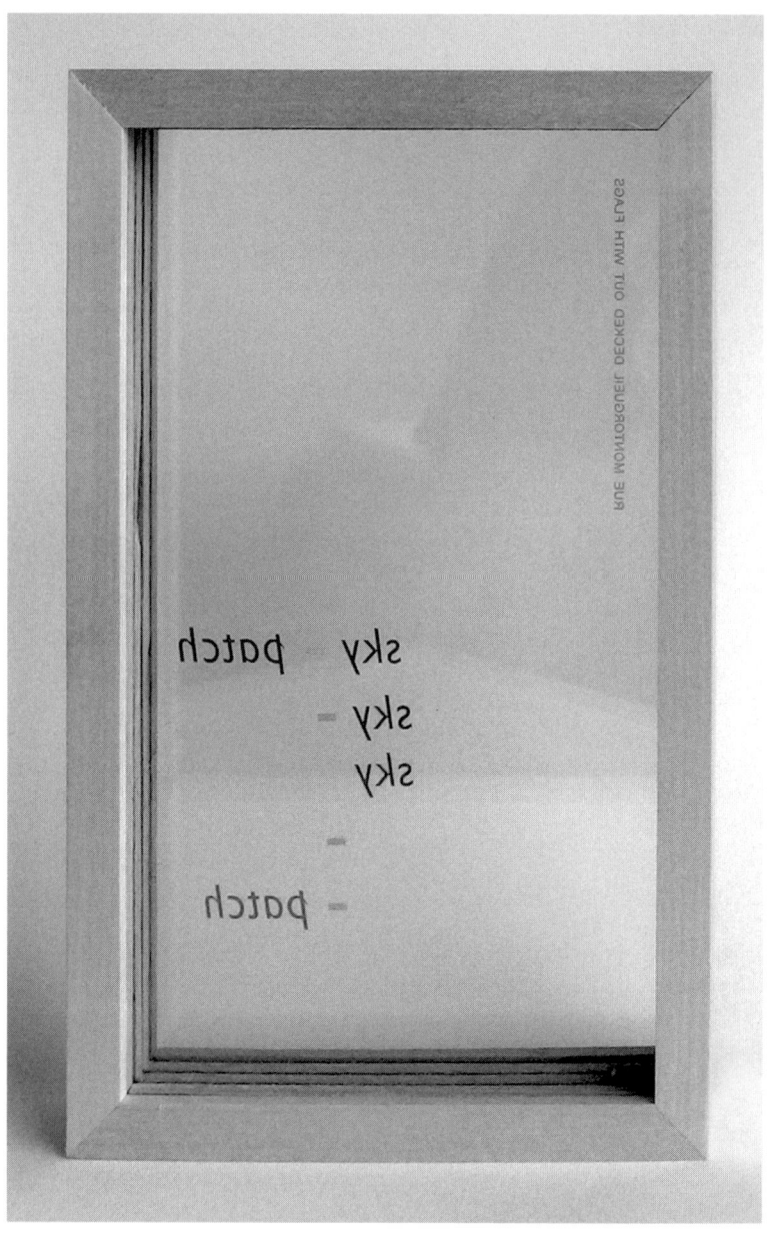
Rue Montorgueil Decked Out with Flags, sand-blasted and painted glass, 1971/2006.

In 1984 I made a book called *mirroirs* (below) which actually has endpapers made from mirrored paper. You could buy such material then and I think maybe you still can. *mirroirs* is a little narrative, which works only from the back of the book. So everything goes on at the back of the book. And it's a story about a "mirror" which turns

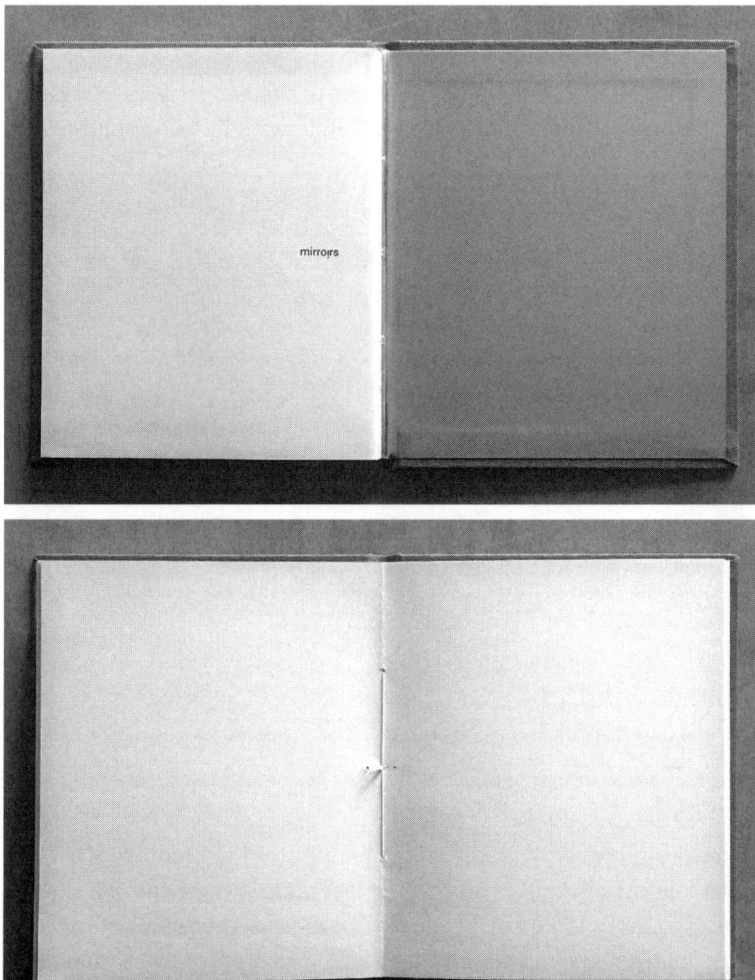

mirroirs, Coracle Press, 1984.

to "window", which turns to "minnow", which turns to "willow", which turns to a "pebble" being thrown into the middle of the book. A "ripple" forms in the centre of the book, and the ripple goes outward on the centrefold, and in the very middle of the book is the pebble which has been thrown, but it's really a full-point. I had seen

THE METAPHOR BOOKS 41

this narrative unfold as I watched a person reading a book through the window of a train. I realised that everything was happening from the back of the book, in fact. And so I thought that maybe this represented a metaphorical situation that I could physically construct as a book. This became *mirrors*, even the title page of which is actually printed backwards so that it reflects in the mirrored endpapers. My own signature was made into a rubber stamp so I could stamp it backwards. Even the address of the press is printed backwards as the colophon and then the whole front part of the book is empty because it's all going to happen after the centrefold with its two pebbles.

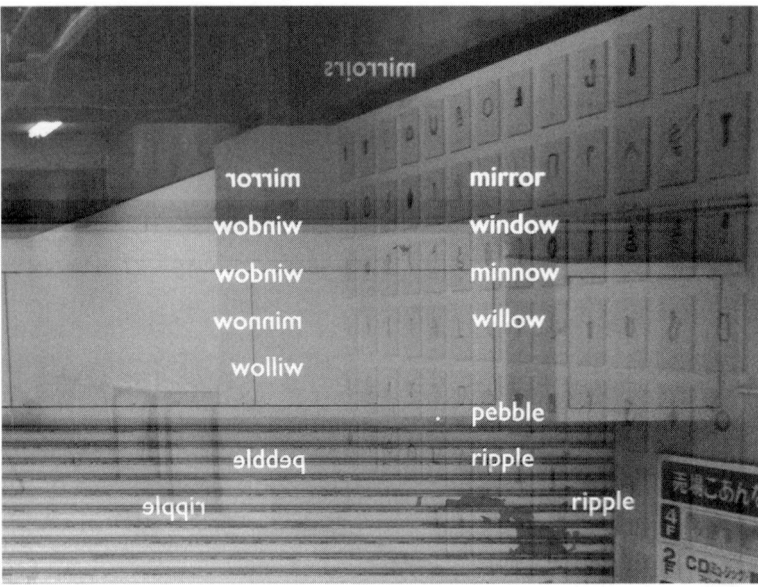

mirroirs, window installation, 'Brancusi's Sewing Box & Other works', Minatomachi Art Table, Nagoya, 2016.

In the eighties and nineties I was perhaps writing more of the 'lyrical' poems of the kind I was reading last night. I think the collections that came from Jargon and Granary Books were the poems of the intervening years and poems that didn't necessarily have a metaphoric extension to an object. In the mid-eighties Coracle Press was really busy. We had an even bigger platen press and more facilities, and Coracle at that time was working as a kind of collective organisation. We gained a lot of expertise—I wouldn't say that's exactly the right word—but we accumulated a lot of ideas about how we could produce stuff. There isn't a continuous history of my 'metaphor' books. They are just pickings and assemblings from the whole of Coracle production.

So we now move to 1990, when I suggested to Ian Hamilton Finlay that we might make an exhibition together in a particular space in the middle of France, in Nevers. I had started to make odd small works in neon before this time and Finlay had already made very beautiful pieces in neon too. There was a work of mine which was a translation of a line by Mallarmé, "a line of thin pale blue". Finlay was working at this time on many things to do with the French Revolution, and he had a work called *a line of thin pale red*, a much more dramatic work than my line from Mallarmé: "a line of thin pale red" taken also from a poem by André Chénier, was in fact the red thread that the tricoteuses wore around their necks as they watched people being guillotined.

We were faced with a really strange space in Nevers, which was just a corridor, and we wanted to place the two pieces so that there would only be the inflected light from the blue and from the red. You would never see both pieces at the same time, the corridor was so narrow. Then I spoke with Colin Sackett about how would we make a catalogue for this exhibition dealing with the problem, two things that cannot be seen together at the same time. He came up with this really ingenious format, which is based on opening out gatefolds.

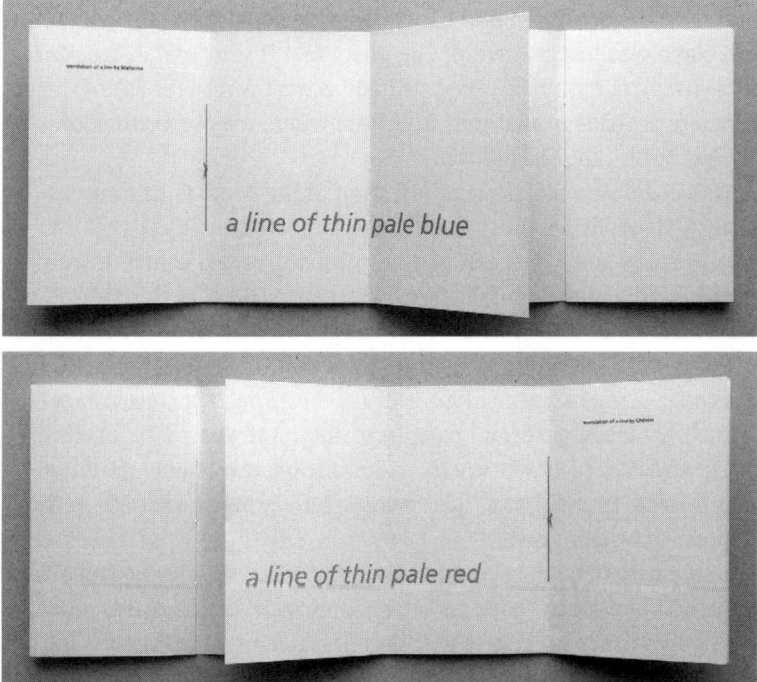

Simon Cutts & Ian Hamilton Finlay; commentaries Stephen Bann, *lines of thin pale blue and red*, APAC Centre d'art contemporain, Nevers, 1990.

There is a text by the critic Stephen Bann in French on one side, which opens up to my line of thin pale blue. Before you can go any further, you have to fold that away, and then you can look at the other side: the whole format of the book leads you to do just that. Then we have Finlay's line of thin pale red, where the line is almost buried away, almost secret, and the critical text of Stephen Bann is the most available thing which you first encounter. Then you have the beautiful sewing of the binding where the red cotton and the blue cotton are both on the fore-edge of the book. One thing I always really love about this 'catalogue'—because it is, after all, a catalogue—is that I think it proves that you can still find formats that deal with issues and spaces from very simple foldings of paper and card. There are still formats to be found from a very simple centrefold, a bit of sewing, a bit of gluing, and you have this absolute explication of a metaphor—booklet, book, catalogue of an exhibition that actually existed. Here it reappraises itself, and reinvents itself as a primary work.

In the nineties there was a poem which I had found very difficult to resolve, but I constantly tried to do so. It was called 'A History of the Airfields of Lincolnshire', and was a recorded line from somewhere in a notebook. In part, it might have come from the idea of Finlay's notion of the one-word poem, where a title could be of any length and the poem was just one word. The poem in *A History of the Airfields of Lincolnshire* is "poppies". Poppies had become what was left of the old concrete airfields in that part of Britain where the planes took off and landed during the Second World War.

What I did was make a single section of the book, with a succession of the word poppies running along the bottom. That's all that happens. It's just a frieze of poppies growing on old concrete stumps in the middle of the Lincolnshire countryside. Here, in this section of the book, the so-called heads of the pages aren't cut; the open bits of the pages are at the bottom. They're open at the bottom, but closed at the top: the uncut heads of *A History of the Airfields of Lincolnshire I*.

But there's also a second part, from about ten years later, *A History of the Airfields of Lincolnshire II*. I could see what was now growing was linseed, blue flowers, flax flowers, now growing more than the poppies of earlier times.

So the new version referred to flax, and "flax" was at the top of the page, as opposed to "poppies" at the bottom of the page. It's also configured in such a way that it was flak, flak firing from guns into the sky above. Typography maybe takes a liberal view of itself at this point. In this case, the pages are uncut at the bottom, so the thrust of the book is that the frieze of text goes to the heads of the page,

A History of the Airfields of Lincolnshire, Coracle, 1990.

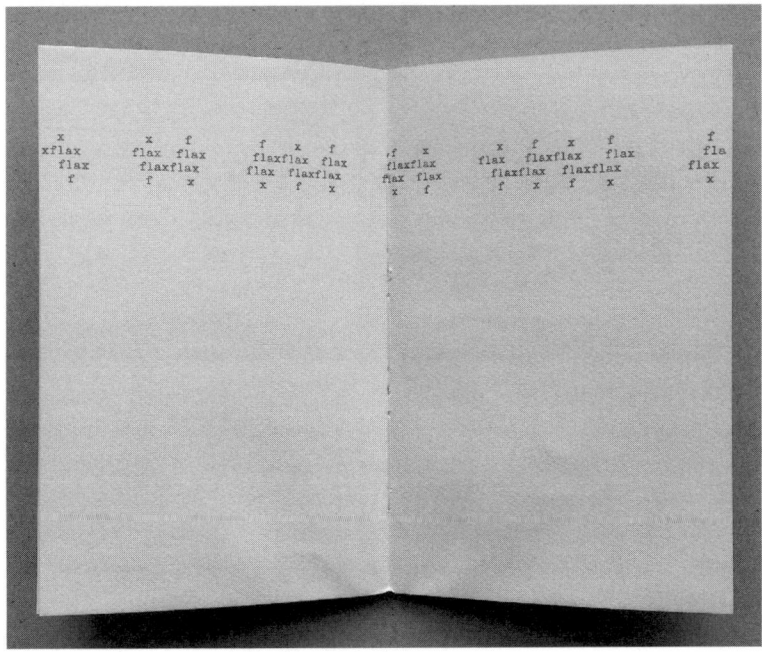

A History of the Airfields of Lincolnshire II, WAX366, 2000.

THE METAPHOR BOOKS 45

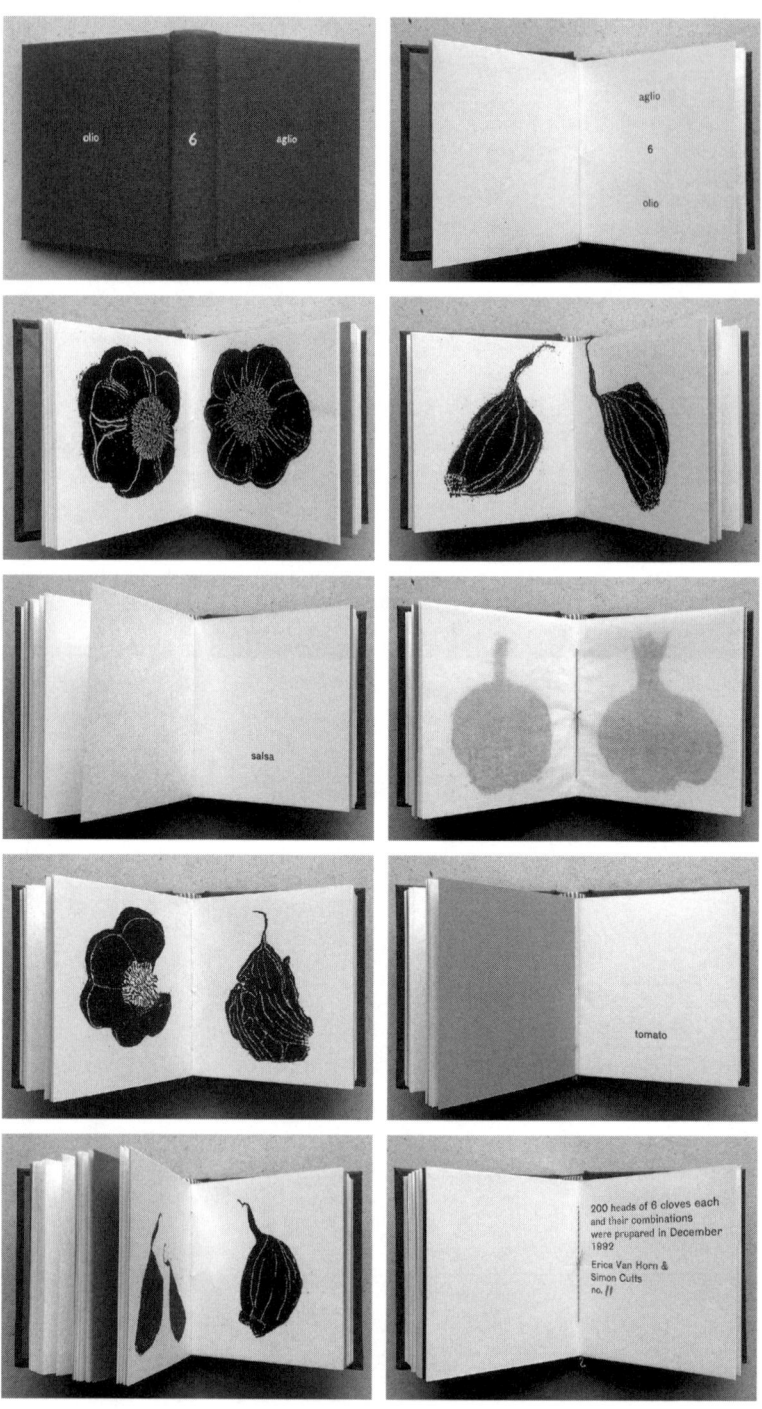

Erica Van Horn & Simon Cutts, *aglio 6 olio*, Coracle, 1992.

whereas with the poppies it goes to the bottom of the page, with uncut tops for the pages of the book.

When I saw the flax flowers growing on the airfields of Lincolnshire, I was scouting out territory to make a work for an arts association who wanted a more physical version of the first 'A History of the Airfields of Lincolnshire', in which we took slabs of old airfield and made a running frieze of "poppies" (see page 121). So a work can extend from the notebook through the metaphoric printed book to another work, as Rue Montorgueil did from its small beginnings to the glass piece. I also think what is really satisfying about *A History of the Airfields of Lincolnshire II* is that the cover is linen board, with blue linen thread going across the whole cover.

Erica Van Horn and I did a tiny cookbook in the early nineties. I can't remember where it came from, the idea to do this book. Erica had done some drawings, some illustrations of garlic, for someone. There were hundreds of small, black, cliché-verre images, hanging in her studio. I thought we should band them together into a book in some way, since she had so many to choose from. So we made this tiny book (opposite) called *Aglio 6 Olio*—garlic and oil—where the "6" refers to six recipes, each of which involves two ingredients. Running through the book are dozens of pictures of garlics, but they're also interleaved with coloured paper, which relate to the particular recipe and its predominant ingredient. There are pieces of tissue-like paper too, to separate the drawings.

We were, in fact, making an abstract cookbook; here's "aioli", for instance, which is oil and garlic, and a kind of yellow colour, and then the next one might be "persillade" which is parsley with oil and garlic, and green. *Aglio 6 Olio* is six recipes for oil, garlic, and some other ingredient, like tomato, which would be salsa, and red. I put this particular book into the metaphor books category because it tries to be something more than just a linear cookbook. It's trying to be a metaphor for itself. Because we thought it was just too difficult to handle or easy to lose, it went into a box, which is a nice way to get it around. Then we realised that people wouldn't know what was going on here, so we wrote a short text which also went into the box:

> Otherwise called the 'garlic book', this is an abstract cookbook whose structure emulates that of a symmetrical head of garlic. Each of the six cloves, each section of the whole book, presents a recipe for one of the classic sauces of oil and garlic. The book becomes a tribute to Elizabeth David—an English food writer—who rarely gave specific instructions for her recipes, but merely cited the ingredients with an understanding of an attitude towards food.

We have a book functioning as the catalogue for an exhibition, slightly outside this notion of the metaphor book, and now we have a cookbook moving slightly outside of it too, as described above. We also did an exhibition in which there's a salt cellar and a pepper pot and the garlic book in the middle, so it's almost like a condiment on shelves in galleries and museums, and restaurants.

Then, again culled from pages of my notebooks, for what might be a more conventional poem, and yet still trying to find its physical metaphor, we have *The Waterfalls of New Hampshire in Winter*. Travelling in New Hampshire in winter, I'd noticed the way in which water cascading from small waterfalls at the side of the road had frozen and then thawed again in the daytime, and then refrozen at night, making a kind of layering, almost like sheets of paper in a stack. I thought there must be a way of doing the equivalent with paper, thereby creating a metaphoric shift.

The eventual book has a plastic conference-wallet cover. Inside is a block of paper, very special found paper, blue one side and white the other. The printed text on it, a perfect-bound block of blue paper, is in stanza form, and that's all it really is. It's just this block of blue paper with the text printed on every page. The blue shows on the edges. The metaphor is enacted between the title of the poem and its binding, a form of binding known as perfect binding, and it's blue in this case.

It's similar as a long title to *A History of the Airfields of Lincolnshire* —a real title, of something in the world: *The Waterfalls of New Hampshire in Winter*. While it isn't a one-word poem, it's still using some of that hindsight. It would be really nice to make this in glass, but I've never really come round to thinking how to do it, I'm sure there's a way of making it in a succession of glass plates in situ.

In 2004 there is a book called *eclogues*, a reworking of an idea that had been touched on by the poet Thomas A. Clark, Ian Hamilton Finlay, and myself for maybe twenty years, and it took a long time to work out how the physical form of this book might come into existence. *eclogues* takes from Samuel Palmer's etchings of Virgil's *Eclogues*. It's a series of gatefolds really, which track the rest of the book in a certain way. Its colophon is hidden at the back of the thing, giving you clues to its genesis. It deals with opening the fold, sheep-pen fold, by opening the first gate, which quickly becomes the first gate fold, referring back to book form again. The very centrefold is, in fact, its title page, "Simon Cutts / eclogues", then folding the last sheet, whereas in Clark and Finlay it was folding the last sheep. By this point, in my book, it's a plain sheet of paper. The colophon is a

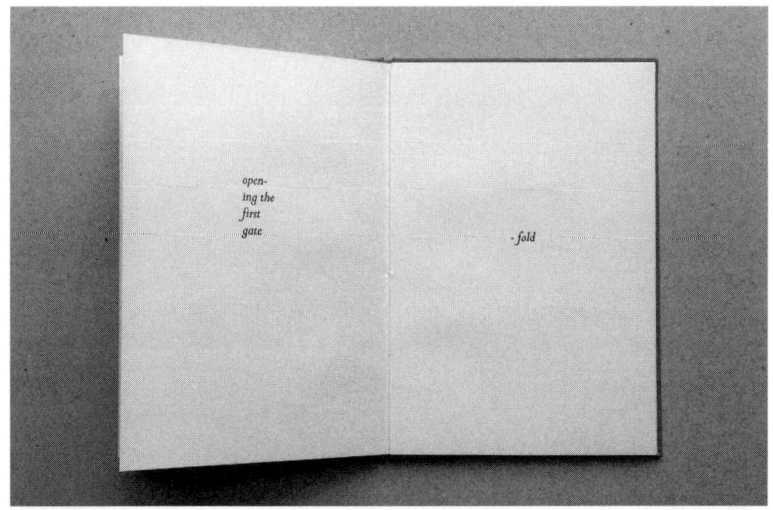

eclogues, Coracle, 2004.

listing of how these terms have been used: 'Folding the last sheep' was Thomas A. Clark, Moschatel Press, 1973; 'After Samuel Palmer's version of Virgil's *Eclogues*', *Pins*, Simon Cutts, 1980; 'Folds' by Finlay, Clark, and Laurie Clark, Wild Hawthorn Press, 1999. Then Finlay made a larger physical work *Hirtenlied*, installed in Magdeberg, in Germany, in 1999. Thomas Clark did yet another version of it later on. My brief colophon gives a history of how this poem-idea had passed between a few people over a period of time. But I think my use of it in this instance was taking it elsewhere, using a metaphor from the possibility of the book, the gatefold.

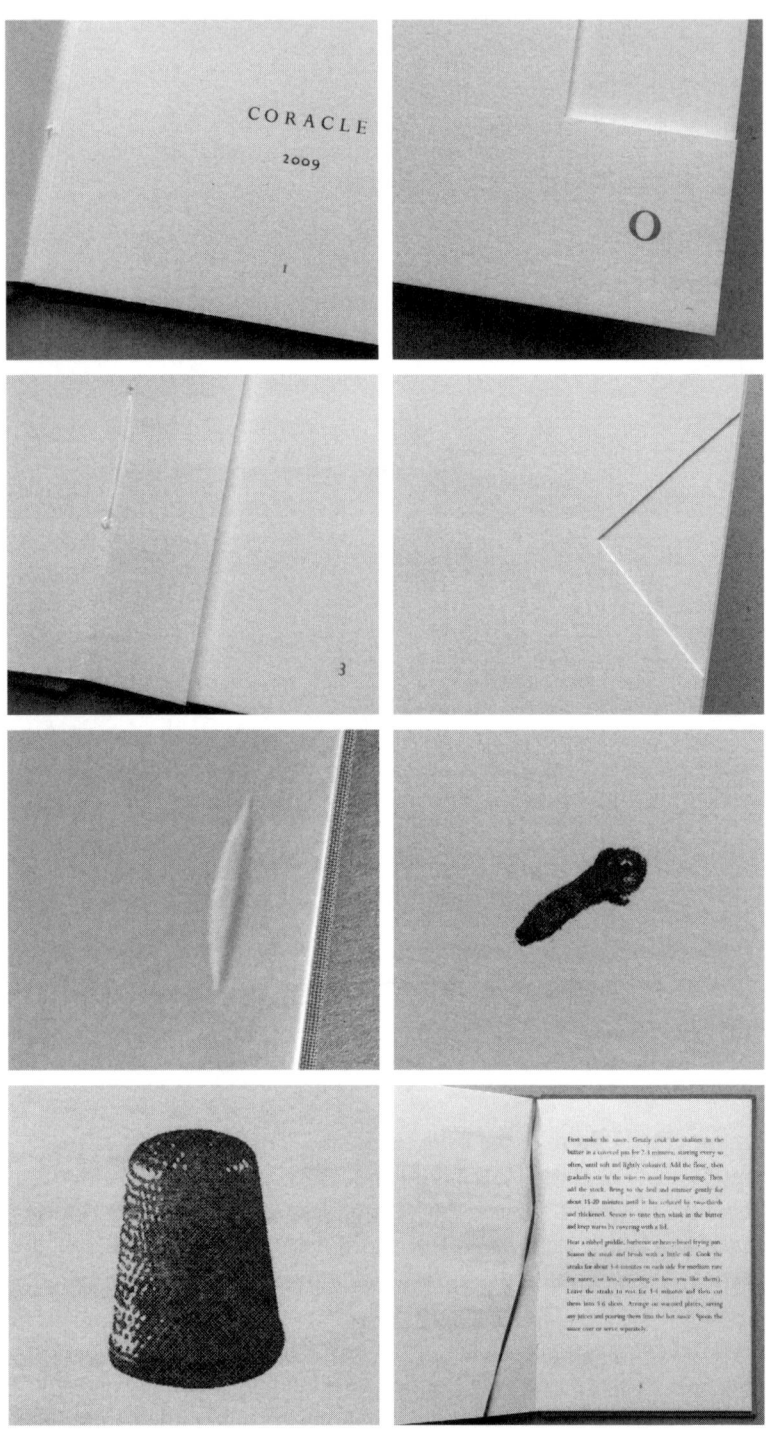

onglet, Coracle, 2009.

Lastly, a book I've barely looked at, because I just got it back from our binder in England. This is *onglet*, and I don't quite understand it. It deals with the possibility of a poem which has been trying to be a poem for at least twenty years, but until now, has never made it as a single-stanza poem or something written on one page. I think it needs further explication. The word onglet, the French word *onglet*, is the most multiple-layered word I know. Here I've got eight meanings of the word, and what I've done is make a handbook to deal with those meanings (opposite).

The first meaning of onglet that I could find was that of the single-leaf cancel. In the days past, when a printer may have made a mistake on the title page, he might just cut it out, make a new title page, and attach it, a 'single-leaf cancel'. The second meaning is the tab, like the tab in an index. I've printed "o" for onglet on my tab. The third meaning is just, simply, the guard in a book, the guard being the thing that would allow you to put in tipped-in extras, as in an album.

Onglet also means the mitre block, *le bôite à l'onglet* in French, the device for cutting the right angle when you're framing or making an architrave for a room. So I have a mitre cut into the page fore-edge.

The next meaning is the *larme de canif*, the fingernail groove. I found a firm who make two-part male and female moulds that you might have to emboss your family seal, for instance. I eventually got them to make a penknife groove, but first I had to talk to them on the phone, and insist it was really simple, that I just wanted to get a penknife groove about three quarters of an inch, and I wanted to stamp it in paper. They made me send the exact paper I was going to use. It's almost the most fugitive poem I've ever made, but it really works here.

The next meaning was the unguis, the bottom part of a petal where the sepal is, the thing that holds the petals, and the best example I could think of was the clove, which the French call *clou de girofle*, which is the dried unguis of a petal.

Although I can't retrace this, I had read that onglet is also an embroidery thimble. And this image is of my mother's embroidery thimble.

Lastly, was *onglet à l'échalote*, where onglet is the hanger steak, the bit near the rib, between the rib and the fillet of the steak. Here's a recipe for onglet aux échalotes.

Finally, at the end of the book, a dictionary-like listing of all those parts, the meanings as described, one to eight, a lexical summary. I don't yet know about this book, whether the whole fits the idea of poem or not, but I think it does perhaps fit this sequence of things. Maybe in its complexity, it's the moment to end.

Threads in Relationship to Kettle's Yard

In 1972 taking *Metaphor and Motif* the Tarasque Press group exhibition from the Midland Group Gallery with Stuart Mills to the newly opened contemporary art space at Kettle's Yard, activated by Duncan Robinson, who seemed to be the liaison between the University and Kettle's Yard. Ken Russell was making the film *Savage Messiah* about Gaudier-Brzeska at the time. Jim Ede and he were having tea in the sitting room and invited us to join them, which we did. The expected bombast flew, and there was a subsequent letter from Jim Ede when we got home, saying that if he had known that Stuart Mills and I were artists and poets he would have been more polite and welcoming to us! On one occasion, sitting in the corner of books on the upper floor, reading, Jim Ede came up to me and declared, whatever it was I was reading, that I was the kind of person who would like Ezra Pound!

In 1977 Coracle's *Miniatures* exhibition installed in a back room in the gallery, almost like a cupboard, initiated by Roger Malpert. And in 1978 Stuart Mills and I visit Cambridge Poetry Festival, probably a most radical point in recent decades. One year I stayed at 76 Storey's Way, the house of Wittgenstein's doctor, and where Wittgenstein himself had spent his last years. The veritable elephant in the same room I was sleeping!

I often travelled to my house in North Norfolk and called in to Kettles Yard throughout the early eighties, getting to know the run of the place, until we began Coracle Press at Kettle's Yard in the summer of 1985. This was a bookshop with showing space above, approached from the Northampton Street entrance of the newly rebuilt Kettle's Yard contemporary space. There was no particular programme for the Coracle space, only the persistent accumulation of new stock in the bookshop. The mainstay of our time there was Paul Lincoln installing his work *In Tribute to Madame de Pompadour and the Court of Louis XV*, an analogical machine run by bees and snails and rainwater from the roof, whose final effect was to give a puff of the perfume of Mme de Pompadour, meticulously researched by Paul Lincoln. It was a sort of residency I suppose, well before they became the order of the day.

Its ambiguity of function, purpose and occasion somehow unnerved the management of Kettle's Yard, thinking it was in some way competitive with the main gallery programme. Coracle always moved in mysterious ways, with its neo-collective approach to things. The bookshop itself functioned as a front-of-gallery bookshop, with various extensions of the typical stock of such an operation, these being

Paul Etienne Lincoln, *In Tribute to Madame de Pompadour and the Court of Louis XV*, filling the Courtier's plates with honey, during the Initiation Ceremony, Kettle's Yard, 1985.

in the main literary ones, but with an awareness of other artists' bookshops that had occurred in the not-so-distant past. These were almost idealised bookshops, rare and often far between, like Other Books and So, run by Ulises Carrión in Amsterdam in the mid-seventies, like Printed Matter in New York, begun in 1976 and still active, like Boekie Woekie in Amsterdam begun in 1986—perhaps in the same spirit, and still active.

    I would say that the University as a whole had so little interest in all this disruption, merely increasing our rental of the premises, without any acknowledgement of what had been achieved, and the enormous casual interest in the Paul Lincoln project. (German TV made a film about the piece, which has of course disappeared.) A short intensive life of activity, almost vanished from consciousness, but whose energy spilled into later projects.

Notes on The Unpainted Landscape

When James Bustard of the Scottish Arts Council asked Coracle for an exhibition of very physical, literalistic sculpture, in the wake of our *Tongue & Groove* exhibition in 1983, it was already too late. It was the very early spring of 1984, and the mind had begun to drift back to some of the continuing themes, of landscape of a non mimetic sort, of time and placement, resulting from the particularisation of minimal and conceptual art in our own context.

The first notion for an exhibition was prepared, with some fifteen artists. The focus of Scotland as the base for an exhibition was an intact idea with no element of spurious appeasement, and it was obvious that we should invite our friend Graeme Murray, the most persistent gallerist of sensibility, to develop the Scottish centrality of the exhibition. At the same time he would bring newer and younger elements into the final assembly.

Writers were invited to expand the context of the exhibition and to look towards Europe, and at the same time to deal with the specific works created for a commissioning exhibition.

In the summer of 1984, I laboured with a spade about my house and garden in Norfolk and on the title for the exhibition. That which emerged still gives me much pleasure. This book, as ever for Coracle, is pivotal to the exhibition. We fought for its format and arrangement amongst ourselves (opposite). It is a start, a way of seeing the advancement that some of these artists have made over the last years.

> *Take up your brushes, gentlemen.*
> *It is six o'clock, and chrome-yellow*
> *has come into the landscape.*
> —a painter of Barbizon

When we think of the landscape and of an art derived from it, we may bring to mind first of all the activity of drawing and painting. The image is redolent, of a solitary wind-blown figure in front of an easel. It is almost as inherent a cliché as the garret or attic for the isolate artist in an urban parallel. With the selection presented here, we hope to show the work of some artists who, while working with the landscape, do so in another way. They do not try to reproduce the appearance of the landscape by way of painted effects. The intrinsic correspondence between the devices of painting and the imposing scene in front of us has been central to our experience of art, as in the tradition and effects of watercolour.

Nonetheless, in the period of the last twenty years, some artists have established new procedures for an art of landscape, and have chosen to work with wider means at their disposal. They have used the recording photograph, the idea of time and sequence to make a journey, the notion of change and substitution in a place. In fact they have re-examined the composition of an art related to landscape.

It would be folly to dismember the flagrant ambiguity of the title, but at first it pre-supposes an unchartedness that for these islands could be taken as Scotland. It is not incidental that many of these artists have made work there previously, and it was of formative interest that many of the home-based artists had a relationship with Scotland. Its use as the site for our exhibition had a sense of scale and compactness that matched the intentions of our anthology.

The cover of *The Unpainted Landscape* showing Chris Drury's *Deer Scats, Deer Bones, Pine Cones, Pine Bones*, 1985.

Concurrent with a critical playfulness in the editing of this material, there is an ideological leaning. We wanted to suggest an underlying theoretical approach, a hardness of purpose, and with such intention we invited these writers and critics. Recent crops of exhibitions and essays have done very little to examine the procedural basis from which the work of many of these artists arises. Often they have failed to differentiate the approach of various artists, and have preferred instead the cultural tokenism of the presence of artists in general. The aspirations of the ecology movement may do almost nothing to lift this work from the coffee table or to prevent its association with aspects of the leisure industry.

"Nature is only an idea" said Delacroix

David Tremlett opened up his tape-recorder on a journey in 1972 in each of the old counties: Murrayshire, Morayshire, Westmoreland etc. The random sound of *The Spring Recordings* becomes its own pastoral, of wind, of birdsong, of movement in the landscape. The work is

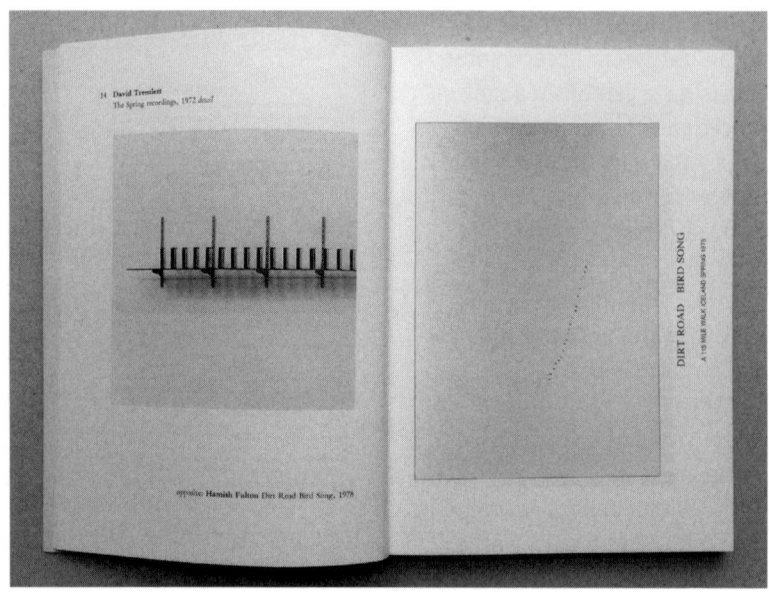

The Unpainted Landscape, works illustrated in the introduction by David Tremlett, Hamish Fulton,

presented as a shelf of eighty-one tapes, each one lasting for thirty minutes. It sits as a silent wallwork, referring to its source and its potential replay.

It reminds me of the absence of particularised composition in the work of Hamish Fulton. A work is completely homogenous in character, and the photograph we are presented with and its text are a moment's cross-section through a journey. Although he has made many splendid photographs in seemingly exotic places, Fulton's work gives me most delight when the photograph has an arbitrary quality, is less skilful, and provides a more silent mix for the relation of text and image. The line of birds in *Dirt Road Bird Song* almost follows the rhythm of the words of the text. In *Rain in the Manifold Valley*, this very quality of the indifference of the photograph is the perfect rest for the resonance of its sub-title 'Conversations of Other Walks'.

Of differing concentration, and much more classically contrived, are the photographs of Thomas Joshua Cooper. He lumbers his heavy equipment along crags and gulleys, hung from trees on ropes, in remote places. He continues the tradition of the landscape photographer. The redemption and singularity of Cooper's work, its burnished detail and internality, lifts it from the glib medium of photography to form its own genre.

Roger Ackling burns points and lines with a glass lens by focussing the radiations of the sun. He does this in the context of a formal work

Richard Long, herman de vries; Coracle Press, Graeme Murray Gallery, Scottish Arts Council, 1987.

using a printed mount and a framed presentation, or else on loose individual objects found on particular journeys. These can be pieces of driftwood, even bone, or once in Japan rectangular piano hammers. Their place of origin is always a specific part of the context of a work, as is the time taken, and the furriness of the burned line. Spectacular possibilities for Ackling's work have been the series *Drawings from Behind Clouds*, where the intermittent line is the result of the sun disappearing behind and reappearing from the clouds. A highly precise and formal work was made by Roger Ackling in 1978 entitled *Five Sunsets in One Hour*. Here he walked up a hill on the Isle of Wight and burned with his glass for one minute at five intervals up the hill, using the final rays of the setting sun in each case. The higher he climbed, the weaker the rays of the sun became, and in consequence the shorter the burned lines.

    I can understand the appeal of Andy Goldsworthy's leaf-box constructions, his grass-stalk line held in place by blackthorns, his arrangements of the various russets of autumn leaves, but I confess to a leaning for his more urban works. A large snowball made the previous winter and kept in a deep-freeze was brought into the gallery at Coracle in Camberwell in May 1985, and melted slowly over a period of some four days to leave only a debris of twigs and leaves from the place of its accumulation. In the same exhibition, but in another room, Goldsworthy prepared one of his 'holes'. By

A hole cut by Andy Goldsworthy through the floor of the gallery at Coracle Press, 233 Camberwell New Road, London, in May 1985, part of *Evidence*, the last exhibition in that space.

cutting through the lino and floorboards underneath, and the joists that could be seen from ground level, he created an unexplained void of the basement beneath, of such blackness and density to be purely optical; the hole could at times almost float in the room (above). By far the most spectacular of his holes was made in the Serpentine Gallery in the exhibition *Salon d'Automne* during October 1984, when Goldsworthy dug under the gallery a space of about his own cubic capacity. The gaping chasm was then patched with twigs and leaves, narrowing the orifice to a neat hole about four inches in diameter. The earth removed from underneath was carefully replaced on this membrane. In a circle of the remaining soil, another inexplicable blackness floated, almost like a patch of soot.

The work of Chris Drury appears to have developed out of the aesthetics and attitudes of landscape artists of a seemingly previous generation. His work incorporates very different source material and culture from his forerunners. He has also re-evaluated as a genuine influence on his work elements of craft, elements of folk-culture and the work of the artisan. At times his work attempts an ordinariness of purpose that almost defies art. The totemic work *Medicine Wheel* from 1982-83 is the ordering of an activity that many people partake of, the collecting and assembling of items from nature. Chris Drury arranged these objects, one found per day over the entire year, into a calendar of parts, which could be read from the accompanying lexical key. Almost the next work he made was its exact opposite in form. The *Medicine Basket* contains all the dried plants that in minute quantities act medicinally, but in larger doses are severe poisons. The theme of the basket as a woven or cast container, of an active or narrative development, continues to preoccupy Drury's work, made on journeys, or afterwards, involving the dreams affected by a place.

Ian Hamilton Finlay's great contribution to an art of landscape has been the development of his metaphoric garden Little Sparta in the Pentland foothills at Dunsyre, Lanarkshire. Here over the last twenty years he has refined the generic forms that reflect his concerns as a poet. From the Concrete Poem of the mid-sixties, to the Epic of the Second World War and now through the Revolutionary period, Finlay has assembled his dictionary of cultural idioms and emblems. Working in collaboration with other artists and craftsmen he has made the works which accompany the vistas and walks of Little Sparta. At the side of the gardens the Garden Temple serves as a gallery for installed works. It is Finlay's sense of poem and placement that exemplifies his concerns, the signs and sounds of words engrained in their objects.

The brevity of these notes prevents a detailed view of the multiplicity of strategies in the works of Richard Long. That is for another occasion. Richard Long has made work from the walk, from the marked map, from an arrangement made on a walk and presented photographically. He has made work in galleries from particular material observed on walks. He has made works with words in plain sequential listings and in more complex literal arrangements. He has made works with books, from an implicit understanding of their editioned nature. For all these he has often used very simple devices: the circle, the cross, the spiral, the straight line. Inside these forms he has relied on a matter-of-fact placement of the material that demonstrates his skill-less activity. There are no tricks, and the work can be remade at any time. *Magpie Line*, 1985, uses chalk flints as its material. Its black-and-whiteness carries and associates its title in a particularly English way. With such components he creates an order that is not dissimilar to his anticipation of the empathetic form of the organic world, the patterning of drift wood, the spiral rhythm at a dam.

To those I have not mentioned, and for those not included in this exhibition, notably Lothar Baumgarten, Nikolaus Lang and Wolfgang Laib, a continuing regard for their work.

Allotment

> The project concerns itself with the development of an art centre for the nineteen eighties and 'nineties. In general, to promote art through informal discussion, observation and practice. The presence in Liverpool will have the effect of attracting many of the world's leading artists to work with groups from the locality... and create one of the most important contemporary art centres, in line with similar developments in Europe, where regional activity flourishes.
> —From the proposal for 'Allotment' in Liverpool, 1986.

This intervention of a poem of mine (right) lasted for only the very brief period of one evening during the late summer of 1987. It was projected on the back wall of Renshaw Hall, beyond the edge of Richard Long's *Stone Field* which occupied the whole of the building at the time, having

Allotment 3, Renshaw Hall, 1987.

been installed for several months. *Allotment 3* was an interlude in the project, an interval between proposed future installations. Even though they never finally happened, there was a pre-occupation with the idea that a building and the use of its space could be a form of publication, an issuing of new forms within a more physical context. The list of potential projects being worked on at the time of its closure included a concert by Test Department [which was to be *Allotment 2*], installations by Richard Serra and Antony Gormley, leading to the full rendition of the Allotment project. In this, multiple individual projects

Allotment 1: Richard Long, Stone Field, publicity poster, Coracle Atlantic Foundation, 1987.

would take place simultaneously, alongside a small site hut for each of them, as an information and organisational centre, across the vast interior space of Renshaw Hall, producing a veritable magazine of activity, an anthology of published parts.

This was a proposal for a model: a format for an art activity of complete adaptability and radical economy. The very economy of the projected idea of Allotment was its most despised feature; if you could bring about a national, international and community-based art centre of this scale for such a low figure as we were proposing, then it would question the economics of existing institutions. It was clearly not a climate in which to make such a radical prototype anything more than a threat.

> "Walking in off the busy main street, I was confronted by the sheer scale and acreage of the work itself. It was something you had to walk around to even begin to comprehend... the work dominates, or rather displaces, everything around it visually. One reaches for non-art equivalents: rugby fields, aircraft landing strips, motorways and the like, so big that the sense of it can only be experienced by physically moving over or alongside it and over a period of time. Its position inside the building—a long, wide, white rectangle on the floor—carried some of the overtones of a cathedral aisle, further reinforced by the height of the roof and overhead metal girders.

In the context of Long's work and development, *Stone Field* would seem to be something of a departure, in that his main landscape (outdoor) works—often in far off and unusual locations—are seen mainly as photographic records in galleries or publications, whereas his gallery-based works, while having obvious landscape references, tend to rely upon the architecture of the space for some of their structure and meaning. *Stone Field* seems to be both: that is, an essentially landscape work, obviously indoors, but functioning both within and outside the architectural context. For example, the perspective and eye-level orientations seem to operate within the kind of phenomena one associates with the outdoors. One almost senses the curvature of the earth or the earth's influence when looking at it."
—Ian Hunter, *Artspool*, summer 1987.

The Presence of Landscape

Coracle began, as it continues, as a small publishing press producing a wide variety of books and printed items with poets, artists and writers. During its development, it has encompassed and used many forms and formats, from the printed page to bookshops, from exhibition spaces and galleries to large-scale projects on specific sites. The selection of books and other printed items shown here is a cross-section of Coracle publications taken from one of its most enduring concerns, that of a critical extension to the ways of representing the exterior landscape, or even the interior of a garden. These works were first grouped in a more selective way for an exhibition at Galerie Jansen Kooy in Amsterdam in 1993. Here they are collected almost in their entirety.

For the most part, these books and printed items were never conceived of as thematic, and only come together in retrospect. However, *The Unpainted Landscape* of 1987 was the culmination of projects with many of the artists published and shown by Coracle at that time. As a survey of artists who worked in the landscape with strategies other than that of imitation, it remains one of the freshest anthologies, and one which still presents a potentially theoretical approach to this area.

The book remains the most suitable vehicle for a journey, a passage through time and distance travelled, a sequence of pages equivalencing space, extended by the concertina and gate-fold. This has always been the proclivity of folded and printed paper from the scroll to the map, from the diary to the collected and boxed detritus from a place, stored and classified.

The Vinyl Project

The *Vinyl* project was made in the Christian Brothers' School, Sullivan's Quay, Cork during July and August of 2005, of installations using vinyl film as sign and graphic output from the computer plotter and cutter. This was the single unifying means of production in a common medium, almost a theme of sorts.

For the most part, it was a textual and graphical project, interspersed with uses of vinyl as a more purely inert material, used by some of the participants to build and construct. It was essentially a project for an expanded book of parts, an anthology using the nooks and crevices of a building in a certain state of decay, instead of the page. The new work was layered onto existing surfaces, prominent features, and other facets of a building which remained unaltered by these additions, their presence left to be discovered in this context, situated in a collective space normally used for a different purpose.

Vinyl: project for installation, banner, 2005.

A central feature of the installation was a well-stocked book room made in the games room above the gymnasium in the building overlooking the river, focusing information on this and other similar projects, where books and other items were available for perusal or purchase. It contained books by poets, artists and writers involved in the project, together with the work of poets and writers of Soundeye's Cork International Poetry Festival which shared the space in the first weeks of the *Vinyl* installation.

I had always been most impressed by Daniel Buren's installation of coloured vinyl strips in the foyer of Southampton Art Gallery in England, a commission which stands to this day. Here, by the simple use of coloured sheet self-adhesive material, architecture is altered, indeed subverted, in his *Arcades: Three Colour*, 1994. It also fulfils the economy of means characterised by much so-called conceptual work before and after it: you can take it with you and have it made in another place.

But it was not merely the ambition of that work alone that led to the idea of a group installation using such material, inviting artists, poets and others to participate. It was the small history of anthological shows produced at Coracle in Camberwell, London, during the nineteen seventies and eighties: *Miniatures 1977*; *Fo(u)ndlings 1978*; *On loan*, 1980; '*Assemble Here!*', New York, 1983; and *pluXvalue*, Paris; *Repeat*; *Still Life*, New York; *Vitrine Encampment*, Edinburgh; *Low Tech*; and *Salon d'Automne*, all 1984; some of which had aspects of the migratory quality of *Vinyl*.

Vinyl may sit belatedly within this lineage. This may be to do with the necessary technological development, and the ability now to be able to send images—of spaces and surfaces and their siting—by email to a host of other places. Then there was the need for adequate funding, wonderfully provided by Cork 2005, and the dictates of an appropriate urban building to be satisfied. Here, the inner sanctum of the school courtyard and the passageways of its buildings provided just such a place to discover, rest and read if need be, in the heat of the summer city. When hazard overtook the work, either by freak of weather or by a random act of vandalism, it could be replaced by photography, of itself in situ, as information, as in a library of images of its placement. Necessarily, *Vinyl* was a temporary installation: the school returned in September. We do however have the possibilities of print, this catalogue of the present instance, for as the French poet Mallarmé vowed, the world is indeed made to be put into a book.

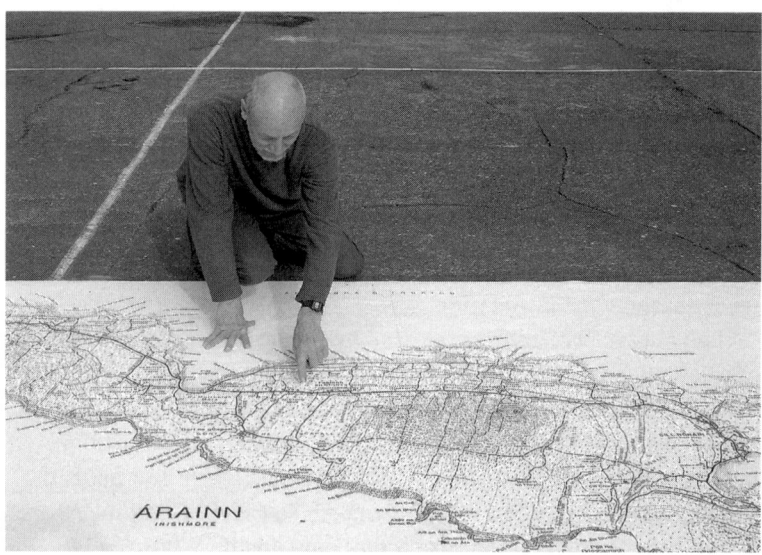

Tim Robinson and the vinyl Folding Landscapes map of Aran, installed in the school playground.

Certain Trees

When Didier Mathieu asked for an exhibition of Coracle Press workings for the Centre des Livres d'Artistes in Limousin in France, it was not quite clear how we would make an overall survey of the work. We had made an exhibition for him some six years earlier of the landscape-inclined works of the press called *The Presence of Landscape*, which was held in a large public space in Limoges. So the considerations became more generic, more about a wider group of participants, than the initial form of exhibition and catalogue. This was to have been a more historical survey of the interaction of the earlier printed work of Tarasque and Coracle Press with Ian Hamilton Finlay and Wild Hawthorn Press, and their close associations with a scattering of other artists. It, too, would have been an attempt to show the equivalences between books and objects, printed and constructed material, now amongst a looser group of acquaintances. In the end we settled for a much more limited anthology of parts, with only an anecdotal history, and one which merely shows linked concerns and sensibilities. Nonetheless it may hint at a very singular development of the book, poem and object as used by these poets and artists during this period.

The courtyard at CDLA, with *A Box of Slates* by Martin Rogers.

The beginnings of Coracle Press are linked to a number of key figures who don't appear in the catalogue, notably Kay Roberts, whose printed and constructed work of this time were an important marker: *A Book of Braids*, with Simon Cutts; and *Estuary Camouflage*, both 1975; and the exhibition *A View Over the Skirting Board* at Coracle Press in 1976. The critical thrust of Stephen Bann during these early Tarasque and Coracle years is demonstrated by the many texts reprinted in the appendix of the book of the exhibition, but this does not take account of a primary work of his own like *Field, after Francis Ponge*, 1972, or the card series issued by Tarasque and then continued by Coracle in the mid-nineteen seventies.

The role of several intrinsic painters is also unreferenced by this book and exhibition. Stephen Skidmore, for instance, was there from the earliest times in Nottingham, and he was very close to the formative sense of motif and its scale of much of the work at that time. David Willetts was also an important presence, as a little later was Helmuth Rieck. A little more pivotal to the conjunction of Tarasque and Wild Hawthorn Press were the illustrative reductions of the watercolourist Ian Gardner. Even much later on, his playful domesticity still related to the project of all this work: his yard-long by half-an-inch wide watercolours of the American Midwest were sent through the post rolled in 35mm film canisters.

In that initially proposed wider survey it would also be impossible not to include Tony Hayward, not least for his shoe made of the map of Camberwell New Road in south London and the premises of the initial Coracle Press. And Yoko Terauchi, who made several dramatic incursions into the constructed book from an entirely different sensibility, in the form of *Terra*, 1984; *Ebb & Flow*, 1988; *Cuckoo*, 1992; and *coil/join*, 1995. These are the outliers to the field, of seminal influence, but not specifically concerned with the book itself and its manipulations. The mainstay was made up of the following:

David Bellingham became aware of the small publishing press as a vehicle for making his own work, and subsequently formed his own WAX366 imprint. From this he issued a variety of formats, from the printed and mailed card

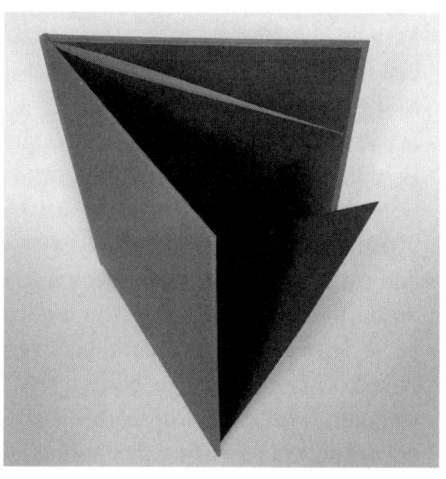

Yoko Terauchi, *Cuckoo*, edition of thirty, 1992.

and postcard, to the small book and small manufactured multiple, and occasional larger printed works. His concern with measurement and gradation, aspects of their classification and found-objectness were exactly suited to this way of working.

John Bevis throughout this time, continued his activity as writer, poet and critic. His seminal book *An A-Z of Bird Song* was published by Coracle in 1995: the tangents of this and much of his other work form a dialogue between the natural world and its classification and presentation through idiom and language.

Tom and Laurie Clark formed Moschatel Press as a platform for their own collaborative work as poet and illustrator. As an economy of means of production, they began using a small table-top letterpress printing machine which allowed them to discover different papers and folding, formats, colour and simple bindings: this was the procedure of many of the presses and book-makers here listed.

Les Coleman's exhibition and catalogue *February 1978* was a formative intervention in the spaces at Coracle Press, where printed material and objects had

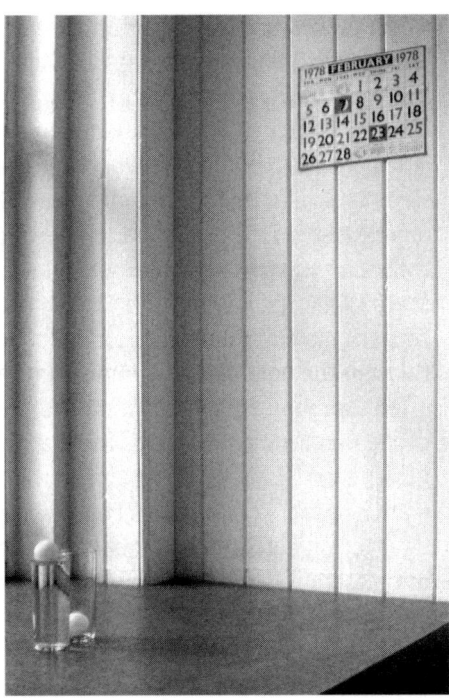

Les Coleman, *Air and water, February*; Coracle Press, 1978.

an equality of presence. The catalogue and invitation card merely announced their own presence and detailed the position of the work in the room. Les Coleman went on, as he had begun, to make many more graphical productions of his work, often issuing from his own imprint, In House Publishing, but it was a fundamental equivalence of print and object that was begun by *February 1978*.

Simon Cutts began constructing books as poems in the mid-nineteen sixties with *Claude Monet in His Water Garden* and *White Butterflies* at Tarasque Press with Stuart Mills, but it was the acquisition of a printing press in 1968 that allowed developments and changes of the coloured line of text or formats folded irregularly: eventually it was the format of the book itself that could at times become the metaphor of the poem.

Stephen Duncalf met Martin Fidler and Simon Cutts in Nottingham at the end of the nineteen sixties, the time of later Tarasque Press, and the beginnings of an equivalence between objects and publication. His objects lie between their dislocated narrative and the material presence of their construction, and at times occupy the margins of painting itself. There were always written pieces to accompany and exist alongside the objects, and books were made at home on his

CERTAIN TREES 67

table: the domestic scale of his activities was always conducive to publications. His City Gardens Press of these years anticipated the thematic ripeness of suburbia.

Martin Fidler began work in Nottingham in the late nineteen sixties, cutting, painting and constructing wood as objects allied to a similar structural sense for print and paper. With Simon Cutts, he produced objects and publications at Tarasque Press. There followed many collaborations with other artists and poets such as Stephen Duncalf, Steve Wheatley, Ian Hamilton Finlay and Stuart Mills. Eventually, his concern moved from construction to the surface of painting and its two-dimensional depth.

Ian Hamilton Finlay began his Wild Hawthorn Press in Edinburgh in 1961 and soon afterwards the magazine *P.O.T.H. (Poor.Old.Tired.Horse)* after a line of Robert Creeley, in 1962. At first he published work by other contemporary artists and writers, Lorine Niedecker, Gael Turnbull and Ronald Johnson amongst them. The disintegration of syntactical language in his own work had commenced with *The Dancers Inherit The Party* of 1960, led to his use of Wild Hawthorn Press as the platform for his own work, and his first poem-booklets were published from 1964.

Brian Lane began Gallery Number Ten in Blackheath, London in 1966 at an active moment for visual poetry and a surge in experimental music and fluxus activity. Here he printed and showed books and formats by a variety of artists, poets and musicians. By the mid-nineteen seventies, he had moved to Camberwell and was a neighbour and advisor to Coracle Press around the corner.

The course of Robert Lax has been well-charted through its many parts, from his association with Ad Reinhardt in the New York of the nineteen fifties, to his friendship and correspondence with Thomas Merton, from his work with the circus to his inurement on the Greek islands of Kalymnos and Patmos in the later part of his life.

NUMBER ONE

At 11.30 on March 20th 1979, Deborah Squires married Brian Lane at the Camberwell Registry Office, Peckham Road, London, S.E.15.

Brian Lane, *Ceremonies*, no.1, card, 1979.

Stuart Mills began Tarasque Press in Nottingham in 1964, housed in The Trent Bookshop, which he had started with Martin Parnell. He was soon joined by Simon Cutts, and Tarasque magazine and other publications began to emerge. The list of publications from Tarasque expanded rapidly in range and format, and it began to achieve the fullness of a publishing platform. In the nineteen seventies, Stuart Mills began his monographic magazine *Aggie Weston's* which ran to twenty-one issues, together with other individual publications and editions. Later he commenced the series *Poets Poems* which also ran to twenty-one issues. He later refined his sense of publication to suit his own needs, also incorporating the ink-jet and laser printer in the process, from which he could issue a poem or group of poems or a critical aside or celebration.

Aggie Weston's No.2, Spring 1973: View of Stonypath. Edited and published by Stuart Mills, and running to twenty-one issues from 1973 to 1984.

Martin Rogers made his first exhibition *Instruments for Outdoor Use* at Coracle Press in 1979 consisting of constructed musical instruments and potential garden equipment accompanied by books and prints which developed the work thematically. The sense of fullness of materials in his objects was often matched by his particular use of silk-screen printing on a corresponding weight of paper. In the nineteen nineties he began the Research Group for Artists Publications firstly as a development of print research at Derby University, but then separately as a generative critical platform from which many other publications and events have emerged.

Colin Sackett joined Simon Cutts at Coracle Press in 1981 together with John Bevis, and these first years of the nineteen eighties were a vortex of activity of gallery and press production, and many formats, devices and means of production were discovered and further explored.

Throughout this period Colin Sackett began to develop his own publications as an investigation of print-form and reading, disintegration, continuity and re-formation, and a concern with the phenomena of landscape and its classification and representation.

Erica Van Horn has been working with Simon Cutts and Coracle since the late nineteen eighties, in Norfolk, Italy, London and Ireland. Her own work began in the nineteen seventies with printmaking and painting, and developed into the portability of the single book, before beginning to utilise the processes of print and the edition to make a publication.

Steve Wheatley began White Lies Publications in the mid-nineteen seventies, and it soon developed from its more literary position of poem and illustration, publishing other writers and artists, to an investigation of formats suited to his own needs. From the late nineteen seventies he worked closely with Brian Lane, whose finesse with the Adana printing machine changed and enhanced his production and variety.

cf. *Boom Boom Cluster*: the catalogue for The David and Liza Brown Bequest at Southampton City Art Gallery 2004, which holds many of the works of the earlier period of this exhibition.

The Norfolk Years

I remember the distinct urge to return to our books and publications full-time whilst sitting in the huge gallery of Victoria Miro in Florence, in all its edifying space and calm. There was a splendid accompanying bookroom, but it was not enough to appease the sensation. It was towards the autumn of 1990, and in spite of several highly eclectic exhibitions we had done there, the impulse would not go away even while I was dealing with the arrangement of a space, a given space that I grew to know and to alter like the pages of a book. I was trying to find a way to make an exhibition with the poet Robert Lax, amongst other things, and the apex of that summer had been the making of Rüdiger Schöttle's *Stadt Aus Glas*, the small houses for which were made by local glass craftsmen. They were covered in ultra-violet powder, the lights were left on, and we quit for the summer. It glowed from across the river.

When we returned, we installed the refrigeration units of Paul Etienne Lincoln's *New York Hot, New York Cold*, each of which made five dollar bonds of ice, and produced a small catalogue of facsimiles of them. But in the context surrounding such galleries, or at least this

The Heidelberg press at Crome & Akers, King's Lynn, Norfolk, in 2010, almost identical to the one at Edward Wells & Sons, where many letterpress jobs were printed during the 1970s and '80s, from their premises at 143 Camberwell New Road, London SE5, just along from Coracle Press.

gallery, books and publications were seen as mere hand-outs, to be given to collectors, maybe as a prompt to buy something bigger. One collector I knew at the time shrink-wrapped everything he was given, so that he couldn't see what was inside!

So it was time to reconsider. By the very early part of 1991, we had returned to our small house in Norfolk, and our warehouse down the road, as the main base of our activities. This present exhibition and its catalogue *Printed in Norfolk: Coracle Publications 1989–2012*, arose as a sort of caprice thrown up by Erica Van Horn on the demise of our favourite printers—Crome & Akers in Kings Lynn—at the end of 2010: shouldn't we celebrate what we had done with them, and while doing it, include our bookbinder friend Stuart Settle nearby in Fakenham? There was a fitting localness to it all, and although it may not provide a complete bibliography of the later phase of Coracle production, it would be copious and, we hoped, a little didactic, a way of seeing what you can do within limited means. Helen Mitchell in Norwich took on the idea as an organisational challenge. Martin Rogers of the Research Group for Artists Publications agreed to have it under his umbrella, and facilitate the tour of the exhibition and publish the catalogue. When it was first listed in the calendar for The Gallery at Norwich University College of the Arts, I knew it had been rooted as an idea, and we should get on and put it together. We might improvise a little within the parameters of the title.

Coracle is one of a handful of small presses emerging from the nineteen fifties and sixties in Britain, Ireland and America, continuing to build the platform of publishing and publication as a project for primary work. They often arose out of the need to make new writing and criticism available in the form of the little magazine and the poetry primer, and to establish their presence. To some extent these remain a model of the activity. A more formal bibliography of this latter part of Coracle is needed. It may well happen in due course. By a long-term arrangement, the Coracle Papers are kept at the Getty Research Institute in California, a long way from all this. The Yale Center for British Art in New Haven, Connecticut, had made the large retrospective and bibliography of the first half of Coracle in 1989, under the auspices of Duncan Robinson, its then director. The Library at the Center for British Art has now moved focus almost exclusively to the white-glove treatment of books (ametaphorical cut-out paper butterflies in glass boxes). They disregard distribution and availability, no matter how hypothetical—and this has always been the main tenet of Coracle, in favour of the rarity of collection. I had written in *Spines & Spirals: The Norfolk Books 1990–1996*:

> Coracle books seek the *generality* of the occasion for a publication, which may arise from its *particularity*: the observation and recording of a phenomenon, the identification of genres, the seemingly obsessive classification. In this they may resemble less other artists' books, whatever they are, than *all* books in general, surveyed eclectically.
>
> It is indeed by now difficult to substantiate any single definition of a book made by an artist, and this very issue may well have already been surpassed. There are only books in an intensified and eclectic arena. Often these books subvert the notion of illustration, of separate parts of text and image, which may belong to the earlier considerations of the *private* presses, and more predicated on rarity and luxury. These new books attempt to synthesise text, image, material, method of production, and context, into a unified single work. If this succeeds the book functions as a primary form.

The uncanny parallels between the earlier phase of Coracle, and that of the situation in Norfolk, are taken up by John Bevis in his essay 'A Star-gazy Pie', but I think I could elaborate a little further on some of them. The use of two almost identical printers, by way of Edward Wells & Sons in Camberwell New Road, London, and Crome & Akers in Austin Street, Kings Lynn, Norfolk is remarkable. They were both small family firms with successive generations entering the trade.

A selection of the spines of casebound books published 1989–2011.

> **Lines on the Hoped-for Rejection
> from the Burnham Market Craft Fair**
>
> **our thanks to Mr Archie Forrest
> and his Committee, that
> our work was not considered
> Craft.**
>
> **we continue to paddle
> our Coracle in Docking
> as if it were
> a Raft.**
>
> **1993**

Letterpress poster for the reluctant participation in the Burnham Market Craft Fair for the second time, in 1993.

They both had letterpress and offset printing, and both produced in the main vernacular jobs for the locality—raffle and club tickets, cattle-market posters, and all manner of stationery for weddings and funerals. In the Camberwell years of Coracle, we had learned to work locally, and the impetus to use what was around us arose simply from a desire to see what could be done with what they could do. In the seventies and eighties we had used the whole manufacturing base of the nearby districts of London, the box-makers, block-makers, paper-merchants and engravers, makers of cutters, creasers and die-formes that could be stamped in the press. Now it seems as if this whole manufacturing base has disappeared. We are left with trying to get tactility of some sort from an implacable electronic screen.

Sometime in 1989, I walked into Crome & Akers, Kings Lynn, with the idea of trying something in a new town, and armed with a notebook notion of my *nine poems*, to enquire if we could get differing coloured slugs of type to drop onto a plain page. The final job was almost faultless. It was quickly followed by Erica Van Horn's *Jewels I Have Loved*, where single-coloured words are dropped into the black text, a procedure I had dreamed of since the days of the small treadle platen under the stairs at the Trent Bookshop. These were quickly followed by the pamphlet *Palpa* with its linotype setting and thermographed pink blotting paper cover. Such materials were supplemented by plain coloured manila file-index board and materials the Cromes' found in their dusty storeroom. The covering paper of the ledger bindings of *The Rubber Stamp Mini-Printer Series*, from 1993 and 1995, are receipt-book papers from the nineteenth century. During the Norfolk years, the books and other printed objects tried to achieve an idiomatic plainness, a simplicity and generality of form and content, perhaps almost parallel in development to the genre of the artists' book.

The books were also warehoused and packed in Docking, Norfolk, and supplied to bookshops and libraries throughout Europe, America and latterly Japan. This distribution was often the result of visits to such places, to particular libraries and collections, or the follow-up to showing the books at trade fairs like the Frankfurt Book Fair during this period. The issue of a bookshop as a means of distribution has always been of central concern to Coracle, and with the beginning of workfortheeyetodo in London in the mid-nineties, the need for print and paper as a means of announcement, for reminder, and for the burlesque of a venue. As it had been in the Camberwell days, this occupied a good part of the ephemera of the time, with the postcard as ever the main vehicle.

The main difference between these two periods in practical terms is that in Norfolk we developed our relationship with a single bookbinder, Stuart Settle in Oxwick, near Fakenham. In the London years, there were a variety of trade binders we used depending on the particularities of a job. In Stuart we had found a trade bookbinder who did our jobs in his shed in his spare time, and who could adapt to the solving of problems as they arose from our strange demands. Sometimes the book-blocks would be collated and sewn by Kayleigh Print Finishers in Fakenham and transferred to Stuart for casing and blocking. But imagine being confronted by a book-block of plain red paper which needed drilling through with a hole that connected to the centre of a spiral blocked on the front and back of a red case cover. This was the production of Yoko Terauchi's

Simon Cutts and bookbinder Stuart Settle addressing an audience at Norwich University College of the Arts, at the time of the *Printed in Norfolk* exhibition, March 2012.

coil / join. There was no other content to the book, beyond the paper and his binding. Stuart was a master of case binding, having trained at night-school in Norwich as an apprentice tradesman, and together with him we developed the archetypal plain book, a platonic bookness, almost a memory of the first book. He had also inherited a vast supply of rolls of coloured bookcloth from Fakenham Press when it closed, and it was the trade idioms of both printing and binding that we wanted to harness. We intended to shift these slightly towards the critical content of each book: the seemingly automatic layout of the letterpress chase forme, allied to the economics of paper folding, and the austerity of the simple case binding. Eventually with Stuart we began to use even the foil-blocking of the covers as a print device, but far from the over-elaborate 'craft' of tooling and embossing of The Society of Designer Bookbinders.

Even when we moved to Ireland in the late nineties, we continued to produce, print and bind in Norfolk, and sometimes finish on the Adana now in its shed in Ireland. Amongst the first jobs to be done was a change of address card, citing and siting two concrete addresses which no postman has ever really taken seriously.

```
CORACLE           CORACLE
DOCKING           BALLYBEG
NORFOLK           GRANGE
ENGLAND           CLONMEL
PE31 8LQ          TIPPERARY
                  IRELAND
```

Construction Storage Despatch

The initial form of a survey of the work of Martin Rogers began as an idea for an accumulative installation of all the spare parts and leftovers of his work to be incorporated in a warehouse storage system in the middle of a larger space, probably a gallery, under the banner 'A Storeroom'. For the more physical manifestation of the project, all the component parts of multiple production would have been placed on shelves, from plywood templates to produced objects, to boxes of works, to pamphlets and stacks of cards, file indexes, books and printed ephemera to be taken and reassembled as needs be. Because of the organic nature of the proposal, its accumulative merzbau collage-like effect, it was perhaps too problematic and tentative to be housed in a public space. As is often the case, the remnants of the project gathered themselves into a book.

Martin Rogers, printer, sculptor and publisher, was the exemplar of a condition that had become prevalent after the nineteen sixties. He had moved the physical materials of his work to the production of multiple objects in printed form, to books and publication, eventually embracing the idea of publishing as the platform for the work. At the same time, in the way he avoided the side-track, even the cul-de-sac, of the so-called artists' book, he becomes emblematic of that repositioning.

With this book we attempt to site this as a different model. The work moves from its Construction through Storage to its Despatch into the world as Publication.

Martin had begun working in the early 1970s at Bath Academy at Corsham Court, with John Furnival and Joe Tilson amongst others as tutors. Here he evolved a robust printmaking style, silkscreening as a means of closely rendering the depicted objects. Using shifting screens of tone and slight variations of colour, he produced a continuous-tone form of reproduction, to arrive at a fullness and plainness of image, with the solidity and full-focus of its subject.

After early ventures into film and potential book formats, he moved from printmaking as a self-contained activity depicting objects as motifs and the informational content around them, to the construction of the objects themselves. The exhibition *Instruments for Outdoor Use*, was accompanied by the eponymous book (page 79) or vice-versa, and ~~500~~ *Gardening Hints for* ~~500~~ *Gardeners* became merely a book using his continuous tone method. *Eight-bell Carillon*, *A Canvas Sheet*, *Mallet Box with Four Soundboards*, *Peg-Box*, and *A Box of Slates* as objects by themselves followed almost immediately. In another

Martin Rogers, *A Trellis of Ash*, screenprint, 1982.

show at Coracle Press called *Trellis*, an entire wall of the gallery was presented as a curved sweep of beech trellis from ceiling to floor. A sample section of the trellis sent as an invitation, and various woods formed into a larger section boxed as an edition. There were larger screenprints at this time included *Eight-bell Carillon*, *Trellis-Making*, *A Trellis of Chestnut*, *A Trellis of Ash*, and *Pergola*. *Pergola* was simultaneously a full-scale boxed construction of an actual pergola.

A very large work *Border & Arch* was made for the Coracle exhibition '*Assemble Here!*' at the Puck Building in New York in 1983. The variable assembly work of *Post & Beam* was made for the Coracle exhibition *Salon d'Automne* at the Serpentine Gallery in 1984, the attendant wheelbarrows and posts of the piece arranged in the garden outside the gallery. About this time other multiple objects made as editions other than prints begin to occur. *The Orchard Pencil Box*, and a little later in the early to mid-nineties, *Part Rag*, *Plain Flat*, and *The Birmingham Arboretum* file index.

We must not forget the domestic integrity of Martin Rogers as perhaps a main aside to his work, from the unchanged left-aloneness of Northfield Farmhouse in Kirk Ireton, Derbyshire, where he lived through the nineteen eighties and much of the nineties. Close-by was Mrs Ford's public house, The Barley Mow, with its wooden benches and scrubbed tables. Here he made his garden devices like the wooden bench on wheels to be moved around, his prize jam, the end-of-the-year cards celebrating the previous seasons and the garden's produce and locality, and later the peg-turners for the viola of the arthritic hands of Lindsey Adams.

Somewhere around 1991, Martin reconsidered his personal work and looked for more collective ideas. This also coincided with a general tendency on the part of printmaking as an area of study and means of making work towards the onset of digital media and its inevitable shift towards publication and publishing as a form. The new direction manifested itself in the Artist Publication Conference held in Derby in February 1992, as an attempt to identify areas of activity that could be pursued more collectively. The next step was the loose formation of the Research Group for Artists Publications in 1994 and areas of concern it could move into. One of the first interventions was a conference in the mid-nineties for which Martin received funding from the EU, which led to the delegates contributing to *The First Publication*, a boxed assembly of parts relating to ideas of publication. Of similar format was the container of contributions for *The Projected Room*, which were also installed in situ at various venues in the UK and in Europe between 1995 and 1999. *Domestic Acoustic* was a collaborative piece made for the Stuttgart Kunstverein in 2000, while a second development of it was shown in Russia in 2001. This led to *Acoustic Shadows*, 1999–2002.

Martin Rogers, *Instruments for Outdoor Use*, book with canvas slipcase, edition of 150, 1979.

Martin Rogers, *Part Rag Plain Flat: Green Blotting*, edition of one hundred, 1989.

The collaborative anthology of invited participants, *Everything's a Pound: a survey of books weighing sixteen ounces avoirdupois*, was organised in 2000, as was the critical survey of the work of Brian Lane, *The Printed Performance*. From 2002, a major project of the RGAP became the Small Publishers Fair, an international event held annually in London, beginning at the South Bank Centre that year, and continuing at Conway Hall from 2003, and held each November since that time. Also in 2002, RGAP moved out of the University to become an independent, not-for-profit, artist-led organisation, continuing to publish artists' books and editions, and work with other centres in the UK and abroad, setting up collaborative projects, publications, exhibitions and events. Work space and archive were set up firstly in Cromford, Derbyshire and more recently at the Yorkshire Art Space in Sheffield.

Martin continued his own personal work during this period, and from the earlier nineties, the projection of objects in various non-gallery architectures played a large part, especially for the annual Wirksworth Festival between 1999 and 2004. In the mid-nineties he also worked with reams of Ford's blotting paper, as had been used as a sampler in *Part Rag, Plain Flat*, (above). But it was the thrust of the collaborative platform that pre-occupied him. Martin Rogers was one of the quiet workers in the field. The course of his work from film to print, from constructed object to be photographed or as a stand-alone piece, to the finished book, is an exemplary development. At the same time there is a real attachment to the detail of a personal life. That he moved from the individual work to the whole platform of publishing is its achievement.

The same may be true of many other artists whose work has been accentuated to emphasise the artists' book as a genre, as in the case of Ed Ruscha, Lawrence Weiner and Joseph Kosuth. Sol LeWitt offers a more stylised paradigm in that he articulates a polemic for books as democratic production that has been taken as one of the main tenets of the artists' book. Certainly his overall work could be reviewed in the light of its movement from construction to publication.

In May 2010, Martin Rogers and Chloë Brown curated *Sol LeWitt: Artists' Books*, at Site Gallery in Sheffield. Alongside the exhibition, a one-day conference, 'Artists Publications and the Legacy of Sol LeWitt', was held at Sheffield Hallam University, in collaboration with Site Gallery and RGAP, to explore the relevance and position of artists' publications in contemporary art practice.

It may be important now to re-examine that history and look at artists outside the narrower field who have always used publication as an extension of their body of work, if not the work itself, as a process in the development of the initial idea.

A wider proposal could be made for big-name artists as well as quiet workers in their field, and I think there is a particular dimension to be examined in the case of certain French artists, like Christian Boltanski, Robert Filliou, and Daniel Buren, amongst others. At the same time, we could look at Herman de Vries, Ian Hamilton Finlay, Maurizio Nannucci, Dieter Rot, Jan Voss, Joseph Kosuth and Lawrence Weiner in this new light. We should also look at artists who may not have been particularly included in the artists' book classification, like Bruce Nauman, Richard Serra, Robert Smithson, Robert Morris, Gordon Matta Clark, even Richard Hamilton. Certainly George Brecht, and John Cage, in the sense of their performance/recording (construction) to the printed score (publication), such as Cage's *Variations 1* and *Variations 2* with extra materials as printed and manufactured scores for performance.

There may well be more literary, and in turn, less obvious aspects to the proposition of Construction to Publication, and indeed there may be a more generalised principle than we have acknowledged before, so overwhelmed have we been by the need to substantiate the field of artists' book, which is perhaps really in the margins. Now we could even look at the relationship of the notebook workings to the finished production of certain writers: William Burroughs' cut-ups, Nabokov's methodology of file index to the finished text. Construction moves towards its resolution in Publication.

Made in English

> 'Fancy that, he said, we both had the same idea, of writing our names in our hats'—Gustav Flaubert, *Bouvard et Pécuchet*

This collection brings together almost all the poems and occasional works of Stuart Mills, from the early days of Tarasque Press, through his monographic magazine *Aggie Weston's*, from work published by other presses, to later productions from his own ink-jet printer, often as Aggie Weston's Editions.

Stuart Mills in Belper, Derbyshire, 2002. Behind him is the Ian Hamilton Finlay embroidery of the names and numbers of two particular fishing boats which he thought were attributes belonging to Stuart.

A couple of years after Tarasque Press was started and I had joined Stuart, we acquired an old letterpress treadle-platen printing press, and installed it in the back room of the Trent Book Shop in West Bridgford, Nottingham. It began to reform the round-edged early photo-setting of type of the faithful Berlim Litho, and take us into a new world of paper, the divisibility of a sheet into pages, and colour for type that we never could have afforded otherwise. Here he printed the postcard poems from the late nineteen sixties, *Last Poems Series 1*, and other jobbing work.

The sublimated lyric of 'Estuary' written in Nottingham in 1964 and first published in *Tarasque* 3, and later issued by Turret Books in 1971, reveals his painter's eye. The landscape detailed is that of the Dee Estuary between Flintshire and The Wirral on the opposite bank, around Connor's Quay, whence he came.

Perhaps as important is its search for a new syntax for the page, and by its use of subject, spacing and visual resolve, anticipates some of the more abstract work of the American poet Robert Lax of about this time. Its full accomplishment can be seen in the postcard poem *Yellow Flags* from 1969 and later reprinted in *The Sea is Silent* in 1991, where Stuart arrives at a simultaneity of surface and narrative, a syntactical development of so-called concrete poetry, but as an aside from it.

Such lyrical sublimation leads to *Calendar* and *The Bridlepath is Filled with Clouds* which are resolved by the use of the photographic image, and to the one-word poems of *Lines on Fields in Winter*.

Stuart had met Gael Turnbull and Roy Fisher working together as Migrant Press in Worcester and Birmingham during the early nineteen sixties. The polarities of their influence, from the urban obstinacy of Roy Fisher to the pastoral of Gael Turnbull, were of immense importance to him. He also learned from them the need for a platform for publishing, which he worked with all his life, firstly as Tarasque, then *Aggie Weston's* and its editions, and latterly with the collections of *Poet's Poems*.

His dialogue and friendship with Ian Hamilton Finlay began in 1966, starting from the awareness of the lyrical disintegration of Finlay's *The Dancers Inherit the Party* published by Migrant Press in 1961. It lasted all these years, surrounding the models of pure aesthetic provided by toy boats and aeroplanes.

At Last

Some books you have to wait for. With *I Build My Time*, it took about a quarter of a century, before Klaus Stadtmüller's performance script of all the texts written by Schwitters in English, underpinned with its history of the Merzbauten, came into my hands, and we had the kind of Kurt Schwitters book we had been waiting for.

It is almost thirty-five years since I visited Percy Grainger's homemade Museum in Melbourne, Australia with half an intention to seek permission for a collection of reproductions of the Free Music Machine Drawings. The cardboard boxes of his shoes and clothes and the cases of those worn by other composers were enthralling. The sheets of writing and notepaper of the drawings were duly copied as transparencies and sent to me in Perth, Western Australia, where I used them intermittently during my stay as examples of art history. Back in London in the early eighties, we ran a couple of postcards from the drawings, only to be told that we were in serious breach of copyright, and that they should be withdrawn.

The transparencies were left in files and drawers, and although discussed regularly, never emerged in any published form. In 1984, I asked John Cage if he would write an introduction to any proposed book of them. He said he could, but didn't think he was quite the right person to do so, and the project was once again shelved. An attempted 'Little Critic Pamphlet' was abandoned in the nineties, but it was not until they were scanned in the late nineties that they were thought of again in any constructive way. At the back of my mind I remembered that Dick Higgins also had trouble with his book on the composer Henry Cowell for Something Else Press resulting in it being withdrawn.

I had been aware of the interests of Wilfrid Mellers, through friends, through his books, especially the one on Federico Mompou,

Percy Grainger, 'Kangaroo-Pouch' Method of Synchronising & Playing 8 Oscillators, 1952.

still almost the only volume on the composer, so I asked him to introduce the drawings for Percy Grainger's machines, and he obliged with a fine description in 1999. It was during a walk in Yorkshire in 2008, on my way to meet him and his wife Robin to discuss it further, that I learned he had died before we got there, leaving his piece somewhat in the lurch.

At some capricious moment towards the end of 2013, I tried again to gain permission from the Grainger Museum at the University of Melbourne, and they told me to write to Stewart Manville, archivist of the Grainger Library, and holder of copyright on the Machines. I remember visiting the Percy Grainger Home & Studio, White Plains, in 1981, meeting Stewart, and noting the touching presence of two boiled sweets in twisted paper wrappers left on Ella Grainger's dressing table. In an enthusiastic reply to my letter of January 2014, he gave me permission to proceed.

From the brief circulation of the postcards in the early eighties, I was aware of the effect of the drawings on younger artists, musicians and writers, and always wanted to follow through with more. Their interest resides in the possibility and potentiality of drawing to form a narration. It is true of Leonardo, it is true of Paul Etienne Lincoln, it is true of Percy Grainger, and whether the described implements would fully work or not is immaterial. This potentiality, the notation of drawing, has been at the core of many inventors' and artists' work, a constructed narrative that sustains enough of a belief in their suggested world.

Some books you wait half a lifetime for. They arrive almost complete as if they had always existed, and all you can do is realise them, with the forms and tools of publication you have already assembled as Coracle. Randall Couch's *Peal* is one of them, as were—in their time—Kurt Schwitters' *I Build My Time*, 2001, and Cralan Kelder's *Lemon Red*, 2005.

That is what emanates from Randall Couch's book, its timelessness. It is almost a medieval book, but one that could only be achieved in the digital age. It becomes a missal of literary, poetic and more instructional texts permuted by the application of bell-ringing patterns to their lines. They are demonstrations of melody and syntax. For the poetic texts, a re-evaluation of their familiarity is just reward, as is the surprise of plain statement in other new formations.

Three books destined for us from email and the internet in over forty years of publishing! Not a bad ratio, but not one you could explain to the aspiring poet sending their goods out into the void. There are, of course, other projects developed from frailer threads and worked on with more critical dialogue and collaboration.

Coracle books remain almost clandestine, shelved in our barn in rural Tipperary. They circulate via the occasional book fair, general travel and demonstration, the intermittent website listing, but mostly they see light through prepared lists for particular libraries and individuals. An edition of three hundred copies, as is often the case for a book of poems, will last about three years. It is as if we can account for almost every book, although that is only the practical evidence of what we do, and not necessarily the hypothesis by which it all began for us. Indeed, the books are all more or less distributed by hand, even if by now they are not made by hand, and their craft implications are more homogenised. After that, we will struggle to find a copy amongst the boxes of new books, but I have a feeling that *Peal* will always be with us in its completeness.

Book mailing, after Frankfurt Book Fair, 1992.

Simon Cutts & Erica Van Horn, Coracle workshop, Ballybeg, 2019.

Living and Publishing in Tipperary

We came accidentally to this hidden part of rural Ireland in 1996. After bookshops and galleries made in a variety of places, we needed a project that would unify and integrate our making as artists and publishers with the place where this could be done, a fresh space and buildings that we could adapt to our needs.

With the accumulated backlist of Coracle, some of which had by now become quite rare, and with the modest production of four to six new books a year, we could survive from such a remote place. With no Value Added Tax on books in Ireland and still with a book postal rate at the Post Office, where we could send five kilos of books for twenty euros, and a tax exemption for the work we made as artists, we could live well below the radar.

Fifteen or more years on, we are feeling the need for a different integration: travel, the city, cinema, and food we don't have to cook ourselves. But essentially, publishing remains the same as always: the conceived book, its editing and production, its warehousing and the getting rid of. For Coracle, very little fits an existing format, and each printing presents its own problems. Or more fundamentally, as the American poet Charles Olsen said: "Don't ever be intimidated by the disdain and disinterest in the world. Get yourself some type, get yourself some paper and print it." If you can publish from here, you can do it anywhere.

Locations

Bookshops, Bookspaces, Gallery Interventions with Books, Collective and Group Exhibitions with Bookspaces

Tarasque Press, Trent Bookshop, Nottingham, 1964–72
Coracle Press, 233 & 235 Camberwell New Road, London SE5, 1975–87
Coracle Press in Amsterdam, Galerie Da Costa, 1978
Assemble Here! Puck Building, New York, bookspace, 1983
Low-Tech, Rees Martin Art Services, London, 1984
Salon d'Automne, Serpentine Gallery, London, bookspace, 1984
Kettle's Yard Bookshop, Cambridge, 1984–85
Whitechapel Bookshop, London E1, 1985–86
The Artist Publisher, Crafts Council Gallery, London, bookspace, 1986
Victoria Miro Gallery, London & Florence, bookspace, 1985–90
Coracle Liverpool, *Allotment 1: Richard Long Stone Field*, 1986–87
The Coracle: Coracle Press Gallery 1975–1987, Yale Centre for British Art, 1989
Coracle, Docking, Norfolk, 1991–98
A Windowsill of Books on Landscape, Jansen Kooy Gallery, Amsterdam 1993
Irish Museum of Modern Art, Dublin, resident bookspaces 1994 & 1996
Coracle at King's Lynn Arts Centre, 1994
workfortheeyetodo, 152 Narrow Street, London E14, 1993–95; 51 Hanbury Street, London E1, 1995–98
Coracle, Tipperary, Ireland, 1996–
The Space of the Page, Henry Moore Institute, Leeds, 1997
The Presence of Landscape, Limoges, 2000
Bolton Library, Cashel, Ireland, 2002
Vinyl, bookspace, Cork, 2005
Certain Trees: The Constructed Book Poem and Object, Centre des Livres d'Artistes, Saint-Yrieix-la-Perche; Van Abbemuseum, Eindhoven; Victoria & Albert Museum, London, 2006–08
Equivalent Spaces: Coracle Books & Printed Objects, Aichi, Japan 2008
Printed in Norfolk: Coracle Publications 1989–2012, Norwich University College of the Arts; Shandy Hall, Coxwold; Saison Poetry Library, Royal Festival Hall, London, 2012
Brancusi's Sewing Box & Other Works, Minatomachi Art Table, Nagoya, Japan, 2016

was that your work? how long were you there? when did it open? what did you use the place for? is that all you had in there? whose work was it anyway? was that your work? how long were you there? when did it open? what did you use the place for? is that all you had in there? whose work was it anyway? was that your work? how long were you there? when did it open? what did you use the place for? is that all you had in there? whose work was it anyway? was that your work? how long were you there? when did it open? what did you use the place for? is that all you had in there? whose work was it anyway? was that your work? how long were you there? when did it open? what did you use the place for? is that all you had in there? whose work was it anyway? was that your work? how long were you there? when did it open? what did you use the place for is that all you had in there? whose work was it anyway? was that your work? how long were you there? when did it open? what did you use the place for? is that all you had in there? whose work was it anyway? was that your work? how long were you there? when did it open? what did you use the place for? is that all you had in there? whose work was it anyway? was that your work? how long were you there? when did it open? what did you use the place for? is that all you had in there? whose work was it anyway? was that your work? how long were you there? when did it open? what did you use the place for? is that all you had in there? whose work was it anyway? was that your work? how long were you there? when did it open? what did you use the place for? is that all you had in there? whose work was it anyway? was that your work? how long were you there?

Coracle: Camberwell Liverpool Docking Limehouse Whitechapel 1975–1998, postcard, 1999.

Equivalent Spaces

'On the flapability of the pamphlet',
'Typewriter Art', 'Liable To Be Anywhere',
and 'The Small Publishers Fair' are previously
unpublished.

'To Climb Through A Hole in A Postcard', 'The
Format of the Small Shop', 'The Poem Itself',
and 'A Case for Books' appeared in similar
versions in the online journal 'Notes from an
Urban Hibernation', Paris 2014–19.

'A Concertina of Concertinas' was printed as
the introduction to this folding catalogue
(right), Coracle, 2018.

On the flapability of the pamphlet

You can always tell the rightness of purpose of a pamphlet, the way it controls the draught between its pages, like an instrument, using the air generated as it is waved. It is its own mechanism, held together as a gathering of sheets, a relationship between the lightness of weight of the interior and a slightly heavier cover holding the folded pages. The means of attachment could be as simple as the three-hole cotton stitch or even the metal staple, and perhaps a final trail of glue inside along the spine. The reader is calmed by its measure, its judgement of the weight of turning, and a symmetry of content revealed from a sheath of unattached and other dishevelled papers on a table.

A Concertina of Concertinas

The concertina-form is always with us, and when opened, quietly presents its facets to the world. Packed away in a box or stacked more awkwardly, standing almost closed on the bookshelf, it may genuinely be the closest to sculpture in a reductive way that the printed artefact ever comes. It may be endless as the column might have been for Brancusi, an archetype that can be applied to the gathering of parts, perhaps more versatile and casual than the codex. As with sculpture, it often defies perspective when stood on a shelf. The concertina has also become the perfect format for the shorter illustrated essay, like this one (below) used as a bibliography of most of those made by

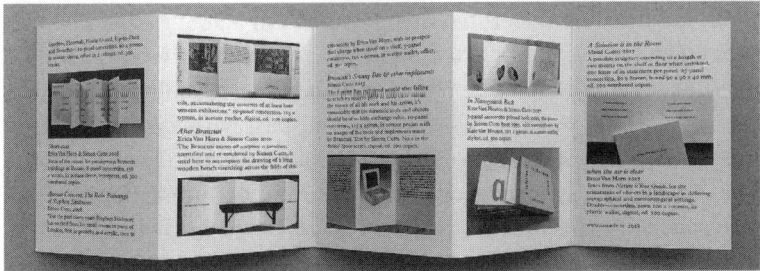

Coracle. Mostly, later productions in this mode are printed digitally on Lambeth Cartridge paper cut to SRA3 size to fit the printer, and their multiple folds grooved and scored by the digital folding machine—a new possibility much more efficient and accurate than the folding to the middle, and to the middle again, by hand, of the earlier ones. It is offered as a reminder of the careful accumulations of Stephen Perkins and his *accordianpublications* blogspot, some of whose photographs of our concertinas in his collection we have used here.

Typewriter Art

The conceptual integrity of the typewriter must firstly be cherished as a tool, transposing the notebook jotting to the draft as the first stage of a more formal page of type. Ezra Pound's editing of T. S. Eliot's *The Waste Land* could only have happened on a typewritten draft of the poem. This might matter even more than the wonderful playfulness of its availability for so-called concrete poetry, used by poets like Sylvester Houédard and Jiří Valoch, amongst many, fed by the equal spacing of letters of the typewriter's mechanics.

A stylistic nostalgia for the typewriter now informs all design, a sentimentality almost disregarding its place in modernism as a tool for the development of the poem. It could be argued that Lewis Carroll's doublet-puzzle River to Shore of the 1850s was a development of an early typewriter text, where the reader has to travel from the word river to the word shore in ten moves of single letter changes. Nor should we forget the instrumental solo of the machine in the sound of the score of Erik Satie's *Parade*.

To Climb Through A Hole in A Postcard

Just to prove it can be done, Skye, the daughter of our friends Maddy and Matt, cut up the postcard (overleaf) along the prescribed lines, and climbed through. I had put this new card into Jeremy Cooper's postcard exhibition *The Postcard is a Public Work of Art* at X Marks the Bökship bookshop in Bethnal Green, London in January 2014. The title was taken from an earlier card produced way back. It heralds a kind of polemic for postcards, as if you could have such a thing with so casual a form, if you can call it a form. Our past work is littered with postcards, without really ever taking them on board fully as a genre. They inadvertently just seem to occur. I love their interaction with everyone who sees one, reads the message, props it up on the shelf. This one is a bit different in that it asks you, if you want, not only to

Ode for the Rediscovery of the Olympia 66 Portable Typewriter II, framed typewriter, notebook facsimile and publication collage, 1994–2013.

"an ode for the recovery of an olympia splendid 66 typewriter originally designed by max bill in 1944 and once bought in nottingham in 1966 with elite pitch and its keys altered for accents then lost in a paris market street in 1987 another found at ludgate typewriters london in 1994 with pica pitch its fraction keys identically altered for accents"

To climb through a hole in a postcard

1. Fold this card in half along the dotted black line
2. Cut from the open edge only as far as indicated by red lines
3. Cut from the folded edge towards the open edge only as far as indicated by red lines
4. Cut along the folded edge, but leaving the outer parts of the fold uncut at the top and bottom
5. Open up the circle of tangents and climb through the hole.

receive the postcard but to do something more, and in the process to destroy it. I've run out of them here as I've sent so many, with its crunchy letterpress on thick board, printed by Darren in Tinkers Drove in Wisbech in the Fens of England.

The Format of the Small Shop

Paris is perhaps still the best city in which to celebrate the small shop. Thinking anecdotally of Walter Benjamin's *Arcades*, and the wonderful film of all the inhabitants of Rue Daguerre in Agnès Varda's *Daguerréotypes*, I was thrown back to Coracle Press's two shops in the Camberwell New Road in South London in the nineteen seventies and eighties. In an Edwardian terrace, tall and narrow with tongue and groove wooden wall covering, they had steps rising to a small mezzanine behind the front display space. They were both encasements for particular objects itemised for attention.

There was a time when publishers' shops often existed clustered in an area, much in the same way that rubber-stamp shops were found together, and still are to some extent in Amsterdam, a kind of *stempelplaats*. In Paris, if I remember correctly, these stamp shops were once gathered in and around Rue Montorgueil, but no longer. I guess that grouping might be said to continue in current fashion with art galleries, despite their lack of specificity.

Passing Éditions Tirésias in Rue Letort in the 18th arrondissement in the north of Paris, on the first of many walks in from the Portes to the centre of the city, there seemed a relationship between the format of a shop and the format of a book cover. The contents of the Tirésias books are rather idiosyncratic and even furtive, and deal with resistance and deportation during the Second World War. I know poetry and the books some artists make can be pretty obscure, but some of these from Éditions Tirésias must win the prize! Nonetheless, the full plainness of their shop and that of some of their book covers has a unique correspondence.

I purchased a few books from the shop as examples of the idea, rather than through any particular engagement with their subjects. I was of course enchanted by the title Clandestinity. The next year they sent me a New Year's Card in the format of their shop.

When I think back, such relationships existed with Coracle. We were always playing with the presence of the front of the building, as a format, as a referent to the book cover and other bits of ephemera which we thought just as important. They were equivalent spaces.

The reproduction of Edward Hopper's painting *Dawn: 7am*, by Stephen Duncalf, October 1984.

The publishers' shop or *maison d'édition* now seems a quaint remnant of the past, and perhaps the ultimate vanity. Imagine having a shop full of only your own books? How very Parisian, and second only to the embossed stationery shops. This role has been taken over by the larger contemporary art galleries, who seem to have only their own books of their own artists.

This is quite different from the condition of Éditions Tirésias, where the format of the shop has some bearing on the frontage of a book especially its cover, an altogether more innocent affair, and far from the haute-couture and its impending imperialism of the maison d'édition. It's a constant theme, moving through the grander parts of the city and the consolidation of all forms of its antiquity.

About the same time, I made my periodic visit to Jacques Noël's little cave Un Regarde Moderne, on Rue Gît-le-Cœur in the 6th arrondissement. In spite of shedding a few pounds recently, I still stood no chance of getting past the first stack of books. These are real stacks, for the most part running horizontally, not in the sense of the term as used euphemistically by librarians. So if you want a title somewhere near the bottom, you have work to do. Jacques Noël knows everything that is in the shop. He even knows what you are looking for before you ask, and I have seen him move titles he thinks you might be interested in to the horizontal pile you are working on. Much of the material in there passes me by these days, the comics, the fanzines, the bandes dessinées that are so much a part of French graphics, the Japanese manga and photo-porn, always cult material for those who know. But there is always something, always Glen Baxter, always some aspect of Debord and Bernstein and Situationism that you get caught by. The shop has been a resource for many writers and critics, Andrew Hussey, Michel Houellebecq, Alastair Brotchie. And Jacques was one of the best payers of publishers' bills I ever encountered in France.

I suppose that we had tried to use the format of the small shop as a place of browsing at both Coracle in Camberwell in the nineteen seventies and eighties, in its renovated Edwardian milliners-then-butcher's shop, and at workfortheeyetodo, first in Limehouse and later in Hanbury Street, Whitechapel. Here its clandestine street presence, whereby you had to knock on the door or ring the bell for entry, was becoming part of the eclecticism and extended discovery of the occasion.

Liable To Be Anywhere

There has been a lot of talk about the Polaroid photograph, its seemingly vernacular appeal in a post-pop world. But so few enduring examples come to mind, beyond those chemical sandwiches we all keep somewhere in a drawer. I can think of the inevitable Warhols, and the two-way game played by Richard Hamilton and Dieter Roth —portraits of his subjects and their portraits of him.

So when I came to examine closely several hundred of the polaroids I had noticed Jonathan Williams taking over the years, I began to realise they presented yet another aspect of his distinguishing eye. Ever since Aaron Siskind and Harry Callahan taught him to hold a camera at Black Mountain College almost half a century ago, he has travelled with one.

When Coracle published *Portrait Photographs* in 1979, it was to be a sampler of his work with People; Landscapes, Gravestones and Signs as volumes to follow. It remained the sole one, and one of the proudest of our books, the text printed letterpress and the colour images tipped-in as an economy of production when we had more time than money. It still has the fragrance and nostalgia of the hot glue of the sewn binding which has permeated the pages, one of the last to be done that way. To date, only the first volume has occurred: it always amazes me that such clear vision remains unrecollected in a more general way except

Jonathan Williams, *Portrait Photographs*, Coracle Press, 1979.

through the agency of this small press. With that book the quality of his eye became clear to me, the tenderness of his report, persistently with the same person in different eras. Look how he always captures the fallibility of David Hockney in such understated terms; and I always remember Ezra Pound connected to the sky by the thread of his white hair, or was it a wisp of cloud?

EQUIVALENT SPACES 95

This selection of Polaroids arises from the intuitive editing employed on several books from Coracle. It works with the shapes, the contours, the colours, textures and tone, with only a faint memory of their literary or literal association, known or unknown, who they are or were. So the linear nature of history and narrative is denied in favour of a new consistency arrived at through the essentially visual. Comparisons are formed, postures compared and alternated; these images lie alongside the large-format square Rolleiflex transparencies used as *Portrait Photographs*.

Here we begin with something like a painting Samuel Palmer might have made, above the Dee in Dentdale, and move through a surprising number of images taken from television, pictured as if they were the action on the surface of a block of stone, sometimes with great dynamic, like Simon Rattle flailing his baton. Or one of the many dozens taken from Coronation Street. Then the stillness of part of a painting focused for delectation. A large number of women. The stone crevices of W. H. Auden's face, also taken from television, and the blemish of lichen on limestone, its inscription weathered beneath a cast of this season's leaves. Composers, painters, writers, until a medallion on a plastic milk crate commemorates an imagist poet. Celtic foliation in sandstone against contemporary bodies in repose; the mottled complexion of leaves. Ray and Mary Moore eating ice cream roses.

Finally, through the text and its indexed footnotes, the erudition of this journey is revealed. Jonathan Williams is collecting our culture for us, since we've not the time or the eye to focus and condense it ourselves. The particularity of this information in a random slice through literally thousands of images may well be more digestible for us than the complete body of the work at this point!

The Poem Itself

I thought I'd like to have with me a copy of Stanley Burnshaw's 1960 book *The Poem Itself* but realised the battered paperback I had was left in some obscure place. So I sent for one and received this almost edible oatmeal version, an American edition. It was a really important book for me, presenting those nineteenth-century French poets to me in a way I could not have previously understood. Not so much in translation, but more in dissection. At the same time it is comforting to have the plasticity of the volume around, almost like a favourite coat. There is an unfathomable certainty in its title, which I feel reassured by.

Stanley Burnshaw, *The Poem Itself*, Holt, Rinehart and Winston, 1960.

The Small Publishers Fair

I think a sense of a new economic community may be demonstrated by the Small Publishers Fair held annually at the Conway Hall in Bloomsbury, which began in 2002 and was continued by Helen Mitchell from 2012. Thanks for this are due to the ground work done by Martin Rogers and other Research Group for Artists Publication comrades. It seems to me that the Small Publishers Fair is a model of arts administration. It requires no subsidy to make it work: the money in is the money out, and you can happily forget the Arts Council and filling in application forms. Of course the whole enterprise is necessarily limited by corrective scale, and if you can only get fifty tables into the Conway Hall, then you have the requisite number of publishers. You can persuade a publisher not to come one year, or suggest sharing a table, but there is a finite size to it. The New York Art Book Fair is overpowering with ten thousand visitors on the Saturday. The Small Publishers is almost a family affair by comparison, and long may it remain so, by far the favourite. Clearly there may eventually be issues of demand, but so far this has not been a problem. It should never really become a matter of 'selection', because it seems like its form of self-selection has been adequate, with tables shared on a first come, first served basis.

A Case for Books

At a nearby gallery in the fashionably dubbed Haut Marais (mfc-michele didier, 66 rue Notre-Dame de Nazareth, 75003 Paris), our friend Didier Mathieu, from the Centre des Livres d'Artistes, has laid out a book exhibition entitled *récits / écrits*. It is a display of formative work by formative women artists, largely American, from the heyday of the self-published democratic book or printed format. But almost at a tangent to the content of the publications, is a clarity and assurance of the value of the display of printed forms. This is not often the case. I think that most of us working with such material feel very ambiguous and conflicted about putting books under glass, or on the wall in frames. They are meant to be held, turned, closed and re-opened, and an exhibition by its nature prevents this, except as a memory of such activity in the mind.

Didier Mathieu has always had a most concise idea about how bookshows should be done, but this is outstanding, even to the point of hanging pages and centrefolds on the wall. They slightly articulate in the movement of air in the space, just as Mallarmé's newspaper

récits / écrits, selected by Didier Mathieu; work by Martine Aballéa, Eleanor Antin, Ida Applebroog, Barbara Bloom, Mirtha Dermisache, Marianne Mispelaëre, Martha Rosler, Carolee Schneemann, Athena Tacha, Martha Wilson; mfc-michèle didier, Paris, 24th February–22nd April 2017.

reader in the garden is interrupted by a flying insect, and incorporates it into the narrative.

It is far from another exhibition visited recently, *L'Esprit du Bauhaus*, at the Musée des Arts Décoratif, where the overcrowding, and an often problematic thesis and history, should have been kept in a book and not placed in vitrines nor on plinths under glass domes. Nothing could have been further from *l'esprit*. By contrast Didier Mathieu's display animated itself from within, a firm extension of the reductive clarity of that early modernist school.

Particular Dislocations

'Brancusi's Sewing Box' was published as the text to this concertina-format catalogue, Coracle, 2013.

'The Rain Paintings of Stephen Skidmore', was published in *Avenue Crescent: The Rain Paintings of Stephen Skidmore*, Galerie Hubert Winter / Coracle, 2011.

'The Two Stephens', 'The Pencils of Matsutani', 'Pangaea', 'Starting from Home', 'The Material Language of Carl Andre', and 'Drinking Sculpture' appeared in the online journal 'Notes from an Urban Hibernation', Paris, 2014–19.

'Some Lacunae in Relationship to Brian Lane' was included in *The Printed Performance: Brian Lane Works 1966-99*, RGAP, 2001.

'Anglophone Digressions' was a contribution to an online Jonathan Williams feature in *Jacket* 38, 2009.

'Ian Gardner' was published as an obituary in *Art Monthly* 429, September 2019.

'In the Shadow of Bill Culbert' was published in parts in *Bill Culbert: Selected Works 1968-1986*, ICA, 1986; *Bill Culbert: State of Light*, Peer Arts, 2009; and *Art Monthly* 427, June 2019.

'Working with Roger Ackling' was included as 'Roger Ackling's Furniture' in *Roger Ackling: Between the Lines*, Occasional Papers, 2015.

'A History of the Airfields of Lincolnshire', 'The Vertical Earth Kilometer', and 'Wartesaal' appeared in the online journal 'workfortheeyetodo', 2019.

An earlier version of 'Some Notes on Affinity' was published in *Affinity*, Coracle / Peter Foolen Editions, 2011.

'The Clustered Hang' was written for an exhibition of David Brown works at Southampton Art Gallery, 2017.

'Martin-pêcheur' was included in *Construction Storage Despatch: Martin Rogers*, Coracle, 2015.

'Notes on the work of Sol LeWitt' is from a talk given at the conference *Artists Publications and the Legacy of Sol LeWitt*, Site Gallery, 2010.

'Unique Forms of Continuity in Space' was published in the book of this title about the series of works by Maud Cotter, Coracle, 2020.

Brancusi's Sewing Box

All the domestic objects mentioned here were listed, with many others, in a saleroom catalogue of the incidental artefacts of Constantin Brancusi. They were used by him in his studio between 1923 and 1957, and then given to Alexandre Istrati and Natalia Dumitresco after he became friends with them in 1947, and continued to be used by them too in their daily lives. With their sale at the auction house Artcurial in Paris, in late November 2010, it was really noticeable how little monetary value was placed on these artefacts. The Lemon Squeezer, for example, was sold for 638 euros. The Sewing Box (below left) was made in 1950, quite late on, suggesting that his domestic circumstances had not changed since his Darkroom Light (below right) of 1930 or his Pipe of 1934. Brancusi was always fascinated by photography and understood how important it was to him. A camera with large plates was always in the studio, ready for use.

The Sewing Box itself remained unsold after failing to reach its reserve price of a thousand euros: given the nature of all his work and his axiomatic All Sculpture is Furniture, it is incredible that his homemade tools and accoutrements should be valued at so little.

I was on my way to purchase the unsold Sewing Box kept in the basement of Artcurial, the auctioneer, on the Champs Élysées, when the topic of its ownership was reconsidered. A book or printed record of these tools could be made for much less, and the need to own them replaced by an understanding of what they might have been in his life.

The clarity of these objects remains undefinable stylistically as artworks, maybe even disregarded. But they are pure sculpture and exist with the certain disposition of his sensibility, his way of life, of having been made and used by him.

The Rain Paintings of Stephen Skidmore

For the past thirty years, Stephen Skidmore has worked from his small room, first in gouache and acrylic, then in oils, accumulating the contents of at least four unseen exhibitions. In the early days, his landlady told him he couldn't have pictures on the walls, so he kept them under his bed. When he did occasionally bring them out, he would display them by means of a plastic suction hook that could easily be removed from the wall, but sometimes brought the plaster down with it. Now it's too late for that.

We met in the heady days of conceptualism at Nottingham School of Art, where there was no course to speak of, and certainly no instruction in painting. I remember well that in 1970, Stephen Skidmore built a café in a side studio at the college, and served vernacular fare, the bacon butty, the sausage and tomato sandwich, with mugs of tea and instant coffee, for several weeks before the health and safety department closed him down. All the internationalists around thought this was directly influenced by Gordon Matta Clark and Les Levine, but how could he have heard of them? Really it was just the full-English. At the end of each day, Steve went home to his room and learned how to paint by himself.

He has made shows with Rüdiger Schöttle and Jörg Johnen, and Laure Genillard amongst others, and he has participated in many a group show. When the sculptor Tony Cragg saw one of his plastic bottle paintings in the mid-eighties, Tony said he would get Steve to do all his documentation! Those sequences of bottles preoccupied him for a long time, maybe a full twenty-five years, until a new group of pictures of commuters in transit, *Late in the Afternoon*.

Stephen Skidmore needs a break from his relentless accumulation of pictures. His bedsitter is in Avenue Crescent in Acton, West London, the archetypal suburban curve of a street, almost a cul-de-sac. It is now ironically renamed 'studio apartment' for rental purposes, and from here he has recently painted the distorted scene through the rain falling down his windows. With the diffusion of bathroom glass, there is at least a use for *trompe l'oeil*: painting the raindrop. They are strong new paintings, with more than a passing resemblance to the late Sickert in the broad brush-work, and even in their subject. Yet as usual they relate more to the sequence and seriality engendered through photography and film, the serial figuration of his friends Michael Van Offen and Wolfgang Koethe.

He is the model if not the cartoon of what we know exists as the garret-artist, but he has always been almost contemporary in the

Stephen Skidmore, *Rain Painting: Two Cars*, 2008.

best sense of painting, the sense of Baudelaire's *The Painter of Modern Life*. But it may be that in this distance he has the proper space and consideration to continue to look out of his window at the rain falling in Acton.

There has always been a lot of rain in art from impressionism and after, especially in music and verse, perhaps slightly less in painting. I remember once characterising Claude Debussy's *Jardins Sous la Pluie* from his 'Estampes' of 1903 as

> The arabesque parade
> of umbrellas and gardens
> in the rain, where flowers
> are unmentioned in their colour
> the town is so grey

Debussy's *De Soir* is a constant reminder of Sunday and the suburban weekend, after the commuting in the trains on the weekdays. It has the particular melancholy of *The Rain Paintings*: after all, the weekday activities of the commuters from these houses were celebrated in the paintings of *Late in the Afternoon*. It is easy to associate the languorous silence of those pictures with that of *The Rain Paintings* when you see and realise where they were made.

Stephen Skidmore, *Rain Painting: Spring*, 2008.

At one time Jules Laforgue seemed to be constantly referring to the tyranny of Sunday and its afternoon: "Complainte d'un certain dimanche, Complainte d'un autre dimanche". But of course there is always Paul Verlaine's *Il pleure dans mon coeur* to fall back on, nearly and neatly translated by Buddy Holly as *Raining in My Heart*.

> Il pleure dans mon cœur
> Comme il pleut sur la ville;
> Quelle est cette langueur
> Qui pénètre mon cœur?
>
> Ô bruit doux de la pluie
> Par terre et sur les toits!
> Pour un cœur qui s'ennuie
> Ô le bruit de la pluie!
>
> Il pleure sans raison
> Dans ce cœur qui s'écœure.
> Quoi! nulle trahison? ...
> Ce deuil est sans raison.
>
> C'est bien la pire peine
> De ne savoir pourquoi
> Sans amour et sans haine,
> Mon cœur a tant de peine.

The Two Stephens

Ian Finlay had his Roberts from the past, Robert Colquhoun and Robert MacBryde, indefatigable Scottish painters he met in the London of the late nineteen forties. And I have my own Stephens, Stephen Skidmore and Stephen Duncalf, resolute and incorrigible artists who hardly anyone knows about. Perhaps that's how it should be. They both hail from the even-then defunct fine art course at Nottingham School of Art in the late sixties, heady days of conceptual thinking, and perhaps no place at all for the domesticity of the Two Stephens. However, in spite of it all, they learned to paint in their different ways.

But at the moment Mr Skidmore has an exhibition at Galerie Hubert Winter in Vienna, of the last spate of paintings he has done, *The Window Paintings*. The book for the exhibition just arrived, which is why I'm writing about it in my excitement. The paintings are all much more steely and brooding (right-on for Vienna?) than the bluish image on the cover, all eighteen or nineteen of them, nearly identical. They are quite small at only thirty by forty centimetres, to hold the huge volumetric space of that gallery. But they'll do it, working on my reflex principal of minimalism, that it's okay so long as there's enough of them! Previously it was *The Rain Paintings*, of the droplets formed on the said windows of his Acton bedsit, slightly more compositional in their detail.

Quite recently, some friends of the landlord of the rooming-house where he lives wanted to buy one of Steve's paintings, not knowing that he already sells them through his rather established gallery for quite a lot of money. They probably think that they're around £80, and Steve worries that if they find out the real price, and tell the landlord, then he may well put up his rent.

The landlord himself came into his room a few weeks ago, and saw an attractive porcelain figurine that Steve thought he might paint, on the mantelpiece. It immediately caught his eye, and he went over to examine it. He turned it over to reveal a price sticker of £180. Three weeks later his rent was increased. In 1983, he had written a short catalogue note:

> I like the shapes of plastic bottles. I collect the bottles I like and keep them under the sink. I have about thirty so far and I am still adding to the collection. I like drawings, and I make drawings of the bottles grouped together on top of a cabinet. My landlord is puzzled by the number of plastic bottles I have in my room. He says, "Mr Skidmore why do you have so many detergent bottles

in your room when you never bother to clean it?" My landlord also says "Drawings! What do you want to go drawing for when you know the house rule is no pictures on the walls?" I keep my pictures under the bed.

Meanwhile, Mr Duncalf has slipped off the radar for the moment to re-invent himself as an amateur, so he says, and not acknowledge the body of work he might have made in his first sixty years. Stephen Duncalf, the veritable Suburban Fauvist, worked in his studio in Victoria Rise, Clapham, through the late nineteen seventies and early eighties, before he moving to his brother's house in Whalley Range, Manchester. He had built a table to work on, and a shelf to hold consecutive notebooks from the early nineteen seventies when he first worked in Nottingham. He subsequently moved to the suburb of West Bridgford, on the outskirts of Nottingham, painted toy soldiers for a living in a local factory, and arduously walked the Fens. He worked continuously on the fabric of his house and its oak window frames and sills, and ate a seemingly endless rogan josht curry.

Stephen Duncalf, *Room with Aquarium and Bric-a-Brac*, 1980.

In December 1999, he made the apocryphal statement issued as a printed card:

> With a view to much needed refreshment and change—next year, and for the foreseeable future, I will cease to make work, or concern myself with Art and all its associations. The time is well nigh to pause, reflect, and to re-assess.

About the same time, a record of one of his paintings, *Room with Aquarium and Bric-a-Brac*, 1980 (above), held for distribution to embassies and consulates abroad, was circulated: 'CMS Case Number 106855 Paintings Currently Missing (Stolen or Whereabouts Unknown) From The Government Art Collection (GAC)'. The painting is listed in the decade it went missing, together with brief information as to the relevant circumstances. It cannot be proved that the painting was actually stolen. Its last known location was the British High Commission, Suva, Fiji, around 1982. Several of his works still reside at Southampton Art Gallery in the David Brown Collection.

Some Lacunae in Relationship to Brian Lane

Brian Lane wrote to me and thanked me "on behalf of the world" for my flower which he printed at Gallery Number Ten in 1967. It was part of his open grandiloquence, and I rarely think of him without some generous gesture, an unguarded affable politesse. His energy was formidable. I had just hitch-hiked from Nottingham and as soon as I came through the door in Blackheath, he insisted we walk through Greenwich Park and the Foot Tunnel. He knew that walking was the best form of meeting. At the end of the day we had supper in the upstairs room of Royal Parade and I can recall an almost constant stream of visitors.

The intervening years between then and the mid-seventies have become vague for me. I lost touch and Brian had one of his prolonged stints in Geneva proof-reading foreign language publications for the United Nations. In the meantime I had moved to London, and found that he lived round the corner from me in Camberwell. I had put the treadle platen press into a space under the stairs, and I asked him to come and adjust it. There followed many printing sessions in the tight kitchen of Brymer Road, many layouts for bigger offset jobs on the table.

Then there arose the slightly absurd notion of a gallery, or more public space, which was greeted with the usual humour of veiled approval inside the sarcasm of the occasion. But as soon as we started building work on the dilapidated Edwardian milliners' shop in Camberwell New Road, Brian was there, blow-lamp in hand. He was always there, well before me, up a ladder stripping paint.

> *Autumn at Coracle Press*
>
> the leaves / of burnt / paint / curl
> already / the wire / wool turns / rusty

His paid-job on the Information Desk at the Science Museum mysteriously ceased, and we were both signing-on unemployed in Peckham. It took six months before the gallery finally opened, and true to style, on that day Brian was back in Geneva proof-reading. His periodic return visits were always celebrated, the all-night printing sessions in the basement at Coracle, thermographing a Christmas card about snow.

He worked in earnest in these years and after on a range of his own publications and those of people near him. In those printed works of the late seventies and early eighties he espoused a socialness, an awareness of lives lived, the problems of staying alive, and a humour, that are far from the aridity of art itself. In that time I indulged in the art scene perhaps more than Brian thought healthy, and our paths crossed intensely with the Whitechapel Bookshop which he made with John Bevis and Ian Farr under the umbrella of Coracle. Then we all worked on *The Artist Publisher*, an extended show for the Crafts Council. Although aided by John Janssen, Colin Sackett, John Bevis and David Gray, this was really Brian's show. He brought together an astounding display and analysis of the platforms artists have made for production. I still meet people whose lives were changed by that exhibition.

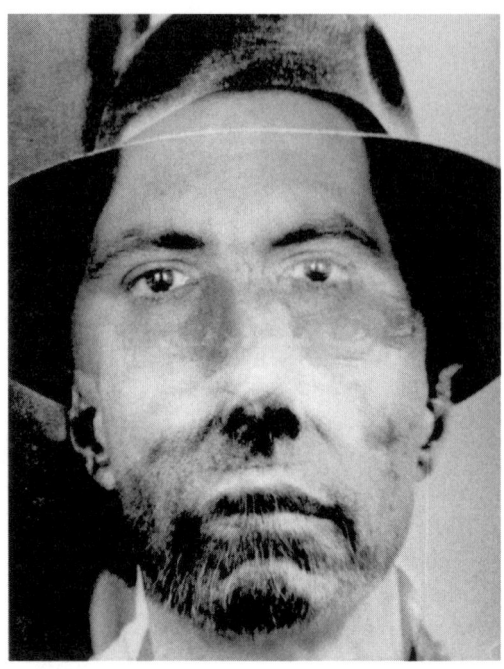

Brian Lane, *Six Portraits of The Artist: Portrait of the artist as Joseph Beuys*, 1979, (source image: Gregoire Muller, *The New Avantgarde: Issues for the Art of the Seventies*, Pall Mall, 1972).

What I learned from him, you cannot take away: the solidness of work, the getting down to it, the concentration on a job. Simple things, but you have to learn them somewhere. From Brian I learned that you could make an open space without calling it too much, neither gallery nor bookshop, but something ambiguous, where other people could find their way to some kind of understanding. A partly domestic space, where there was always tea and refreshment, where there were always pages to fold if no-one came to visit.

But it was the spirit of trying something, from the cynical optimism of an entrenched position. You had the feeling with Brian, working with him, that something could exist in spite of all the difficulties. That you could work anywhere with a table and chair, and with a complete unconcernedness for fame or reputation.

Anglophone Digressions

Jonathan Williams approached England as he approached everything: with an erudite and eclectic epicureanism. In the nineteen sixties he travelled the country from his base in Hampstead, London, in the company of Ronald Johnson in search of new innate qualities that would fit his vision of the place. It resulted in Ron's *Book of the Green Man* and Jonathan's *The Lucidities*, 1967, among many other things.

The valley of the River Dee between Sedbergh and Dent, in Cumbria, directly across from Corn Close, where Jonathan Williams lived part of each year, from 1969 to 1998.

Later, settling with Thomas Meyer at Corn Close in Dentdale, Cumbria, just west of the Pennines, he extended his fascination for what he came to see as a peculiar place. It remains enigmatic to many of us, even if we come from it. Where he chose to live is littered with footnotes from Bunting's *Briggflatts*, names and places on a journey across the north of England, from the Quaker Meeting House itself, near to Corn Close, through Teesdale to darkest Tyneside. For myself this territory is somewhat bound-up with a circumspect view of the North, well beyond my parts in lowland Derbyshire. Erica and I once walked from my father's house there in Belper to Jonathan's in Dentdale, along the Pennine Way and then branched off towards Dent, over about ten days. It was a way of locating his open moorland while at the same time escaping the industrialised, over-populated and built-up Midlands.

Jonathan was always looking for great pub food, but was often disappointed. Armed with *The Good Beer Guide*, *The Good Pub Guide*, and on occasion even *The Good Food Guide*, he thought he might find the true vernacular of English cooking. Instead, he was once served the blackened kidneys of a mixed grill at the High Force Hotel in Upper Teesdale in 1977, only to be drawn in charcoal by Ian Gardner for a retaliatory postcard. The Sun Inn in Dent was his local, but only for drinking. It was here that they thought Jonathan must be Canadian because he was such a nice chap! It was at times all very tweedy. He called himself The Squire and often dressed appropriately.

Tom would often cook in the vernacular of the American South. They had published *White Trash Cookery*, and it was with a recipe from that book that they came first in The Independent newspaper's cookery competition one year. 'Rack of Spam' won them a bottle of extra virgin Tuscan olive oil.

Jonathan often remarked on the names of the owners of the Sharrow Bay Hotel and Restaurant at Windemere in the Lake District. Francis Coulson and Brian Sack were a rather Pythonesque couple, who, they claimed, had invented Sticky Toffee Pudding. Jonathan revelled in the names of all the odd dinners and puddings of English cooking: Dead Baby, Babies Head, Spotted Dick, Blue Vinny, Wet Nelly, Sussex Pond Pudding, Toad in the Hole, names he delighted in and celebrated in *Super-Duper Zuppa Inglese (and Other Trifles from the Land of Stodge)*. In these interests, there is more than a nod to Jane and Geoffrey Grigson, and their attempt to locate a certain Englishness.

He thought the beer from Faversham, Kent was called Shepherd's Knee, when in fact it was Shepherd's Neame, after the family who made it. He delighted in the composer Frederick Delius, the composer being born in Bradford, and that his brother still had a garage there. I once took all the bones out of a trout for him at the Tate Gallery Restaurant. We both thought later on that John Livingstone Learmonth's *Wines of the Northern Rhone* was a kind of bible.

I remember Jonathan first of all as the reluctant compere of Poetry 66 in Nottingham, hearing in advance of his legendary epicurean tastes, his 'wants' list, which as a young poet, I could never match or provide. Years later in Norfolk, when he asked for a hundred oysters and the best Sancerre, I could.

Jonathan was one of the few Americans who could grasp the game of cricket. We were both great admirers of John Arlott, legendary commentator of the game, but also poet, policeman, expert and writer on Beaujolais (I like to drink Beaujolais with my Beaujolais, he once said). His drôle, laconic voice, with perfect pace and pitch, still echoes down the years. I think I read that he died falling down the steps of his cellar.

My last visit to see him was to his Skywinding Farm, Scaly Mountain, North Carolina—Corn Close in a parallel universe, the way it is perched above the road and the turn up to it. We went to talk of his archive of photographs taken over the years. We brought with us, among other things, an astounding Gruner Veltliner—exactly his kind of wine, and with more than a touch of Bruckner about it. He only moved from his chair with great difficulty. The Weather Channel was still on as it had been during my last visit, and the video-loop of the fire was still burning in the hearth.

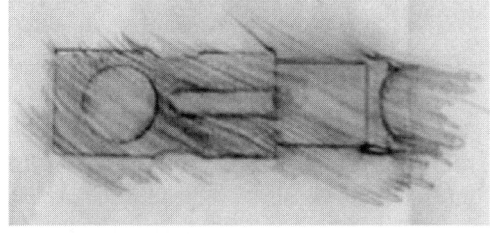

In May 2008 we made a last visit to Corn Close. It was strange to be there without him, and more than a little bleak, but it was such a beautiful day that the valley across the Dee was singing, a score propped-up in front of us. I did a rubbing of Jonathan's cigar-cutter left there on the desk, almost the ghost of itself, open and with the blade receded, as if he were just about to take the closed end off the day's cigar.

Ian Gardner

Ian Gardner, the eminent watercolourist, has died in his home town of Lancaster at the age of seventy-five. He attended Lancaster School of Art before post-graduate studies at Nottingham School of Art under David Measures and David Willetts. Gardner's work developed through the flatness of American abstract painting, which he then applied to printmaking, screenprinting in particular, before eventually discovering an equivalent reductive flatness of imagery in the watercolours of John Sell Cotman and other essentially English painters in the medium.

Ian Gardner, *The Walled Garden, Spandau*, c.1980.

The collaborative work Gardner produced with Tarasque Press in Nottingham with Simon Cutts and Stuart Mills led him from the visual to the literary and back again, and culminated in the group exhibition *Metaphor and Motif* in 1972 which travelled widely in the UK. He worked with the American poet Jonathan Williams, who lived in Dentdale, Cumbria, to produce *Pairidaeza*, a portfolio of images of topiaries from the nearby Levens Hall in Kendal. These were to become archetypes of his reduction of watercolour to simple forms: his work was to redeem the medium from the folly of assumed amateurism, and imbue it with new possibility.

Gardner taught in many places, mostly in printmaking at Bradford School of Art, where he spawned a school around him of flat watercolour and print landscapes with artists like Karl Torok and others who became the New Arcadians, with the historical input of Patrick Eyres. He once hired a bus to take his excited students to the birthplace of Frederic Delius, the composer. The assembled company boarded the bus early one morning. It drove round the corner, where they were told to get off; they had arrived at the Delius Brothers Garage in the middle of Bradford.

Ian Gardner became a constant collaborator of Ian Hamilton Finlay's Wild Hawthorn Press in Lanarkshire during the 1970s and early 1980s and produced some of his most highly developed collaborations on print, book, and card projects with the poet. Perhaps most enduring are the sectional watercolours for *A Walled Garden: A History of the*

Spandau Garden in the Time of the Architect Albert Speer, the emblem book Finlay devised from his correspondence with Speer about his own rubble garden at Spandau in the late 1970s.

Back in Lancaster, his later work took on the celebration of domesticity, his allotment garden and its produce, the kitchen plants where some of the imagery had begun. It was well short of any aspirations or pretensions to contemporaneity. The notion of the immediacy of publishing stayed with him all his life, and even after serious illness; the 'At a Stroke' series of cards and printed ephemera continued to the end, running to an accumulation of more than twenty items. He could usually be found in the Sun Hotel, hanging a few pictures in a side room, attending to his correspondence and sending out cards at his regular table.

In the Shadow of Bill Culbert

The work of Bill Culbert is surrounded by the manufacturing world of functional objects, mostly from France, where he has lived and worked over the last twenty-five years. This would include the 2CV car and its parts, the products of glass and electricity, and domestic ware. His perception of this world also carries with it a preference for the design styles of the nineteen forties and fifties, with their round cornered quadrilaterals and triangles, the flying wedges of coffee tables and the first glimpse of a space age. To this could be added the awareness and possibilities of the 'habitants-paysagistes', as located and documented by the landscapist Bernard Lassus, and the improvisations of the local village *garagiste*.

His work celebrates a world of ordinary objects and the place in it for a new art derived from them. It demonstrates to us a resourcefulness to exist from the found discarded objects of the material world, and its delight is in the bricolage of their re-usage. In this lies its moral.

He utilises a succession of objects which will provide light from electricity. From

Bill Culbert, *Frosted Bulb in Sun*, 1979.

table to wall to the ceiling and onto the floor, they both help us to see, but also manifest their own particular nature. It is in this fusion of purpose and playfulness that the invention of Bill Culbert arises.

The used objects from which he makes the work are often in a continuing state of repair, from their discardedness to their re-arrangement in what will be considered a final work. Even their very brokenness has at times been used as part of the work itself; re-viewed in this way the patchwork of blemishes on the enamel jug and bowl of *Dalmatian*, 1981, create their own metaphoric point.

A jug is also a table lamp pouring its spilt light, and jugs can form ubiquitous patterns of flight across the parlour wall. A table lamp is also the room itself with the bulb suspended from the ceiling, and now a column of tables with light running through them to form a lighthouse. A row of white translucent detergent containers, connected and irradiated by a fluorescent tube, is poetically described as *Long White Cloud*, 1985. Similar yet differently coloured containers connected in the same way and held at each end by a coat peg could be described as wall lights.

A lunch box announces itself as a constellation of projected filaments, as does the indented lid of a box of sugar cubes. Such works of camera obscura have always been an important aspect of Bill Culbert's work, and may have started with the perception of the simple perforations in a lampshade producing a patterned corner to the room. A pin-hole perforation magnifies the filament of a clear tungsten light bulb and at the same time projects it to the nearest surface.

A culminatory aspect of the work has arisen from the discovery and realisation that through the correct weight and density of bistro wine glass, red wine is both solid enough to cast its own shadow and translucent enough to refract the filament at the centre of the electric light bulb. This was the beginning of the work *Small Glass, Pouring Light* from 1983, which was shown in London, Paris and New York during that year. The installed work can only be completed by its use as a table of drinking glasses, for the simplest sort of curatorship of the work is to drink the wine, and thereby prevent an accumulation of dust from soiling its immaculate surface. By such an act, it becomes an ordinary part of our life, yet at the same time a transition of mysterious significance is continuously taking place in front of us.

The ongoing 2CV series consists of paintings from 1960, objects and photographs. As with the previous work, and the photo-book produced in 1984, the photograph is at times a work in its own right, and at times a contextual reference to other work and sources. The 2CV objects are formed from parts of the car; headlamps become

Bill Culbert, *Small Glass Pouring Light*, 1983, Chateau d'Oiron, Deux-Sevres, France.

chandeliers and standard lamps, and they are also replaced at exactly the right height and distance apart in a room, shining outwards towards the street. Hub-caps become furniture, and the windscreen is used for the back of a chair.

Someone's Christmas tree at the Cafe Regain, Revest des Brousses, in 1980, is in fact Marcel Duchamp's bottle rack covered in silver foil for the occasion.

2

Bill Culbert's strategy for working developed from and through the painting of his early years, to the kinetic-field and the camera-obscura pieces of the mid-nineteen sixties, to the ready-made and bricolage works   the suitcase, the 2CV parts, to the more pure object-of-light pieces. Besides these, there have always been the photographic works in parallel to the objects and installations, but working within their own state and dimension. Through all the work runs the distilled optimism of the modernist, his structured inquiry, the research-base of his project.

Finishing the book *Some More Notes on Writing & Drinking* in 2010 by the addition of a hand-drawn glass and a holographic poem by Parker pen, and with the aid of an assembly of corkscrews.

The intruded light tube, the fluorescent strip in various sizes and combinations is one of the parts of his work. Light tubes have been imposed on large photographic installations, as in *Weather*, 1988. They have been installed from wall to floor and floor to wall and through furniture, even through Alvar Aalto's small table in *Table Lamp II*, 1982. They were thrust through the windows of a full scale model of the Serpentine Gallery windows in *An Explanation of Light*, 1984. In 2009, new versions of their use have become the proposition for an exhibition at Peer Art Gallery in Hoxton, London

The three works for *State of Light* are wall works and as such respond to the formality of the gallery, as distinct from the scatter pieces of a floor installation. In floor pieces such as *Flat Light House*, 2008, or *Flotsam*, 1992, or the seemingly randomised *Spacific Plastics* of 2001, *Pacific Flotsam* of 2007, where the intruded light tubes irradiate an organised scattering of discarded plastic containers, forming an enormous glow of coloured light, Culbert reminds us of the beauty of discardable materials and their re-use.

A black wall, a white wall, and a line of light in a closed space only visible from the street window and door of the adjacent empty shop. Bill Culbert has used this device before in *Fault*, 1993, where the fluorescent strip would run through all the windows on the face of

Wellington City Art Gallery, New Zealand, a length of forty-two metres and a total of twenty-three windows on the first floor and ten larger ones on the ground.

The black and the white wall of the other space is made up of an assembly of used window frames forming an asymmetric cluster at their centre, to be crossed by imposed light tubes. *Light Out Square Pane*, a smaller work shown earlier this year at Roslyn Oxley9 Gallery in Sydney, Australia, demonstrates most fully the austerity and asymmetry of these window works, where in this case the light tubes partially frame the pane and do not cross it, and emphasise the severity of the pane of glass: the window frame, the casement of light.

Windows, their glazed frames, car windscreens, have often figured in the work. They have gone as far as the intimated flat-pack of *Flat Light House*, 2008. Besides their resource as parts of works, the windscreens and panels from Citroen 2CV cars have been used by Culbert as more domestic shields and tables, as they are used in the vernacular as canopies over porches and doors.

We are witnessing the last days of the incandescent light bulb, to be replaced for reasons of ecology. For Peer, Bill Culbert celebrates this with a multiple piece in the form of *The Last Incandescent Light Bulb* where the clear bulb is used as the stopper of a glass decanter. The image of this was first used as a photographic work *Decanter* from 1985, and the unique object itself was often seen in the Culbert household.

A recent monograph of the whole oeuvre of Bill Culbert (Ian Wedde, *Making Light Work*, Auckland University Press, 2009) shows its enormous width and range, far more so than that presumed for more acclaimed artists working from Britain through a most fertile time. He is one of very few really radical figures who has not settled for manufacture, brand and production, and this is manifest and evidenced by the careful research of Ian Wedde in this exemplary critical work.

There is always a duality in the photographic works of Bill Culbert, an ambiguity that posits the issue of what is the work: the subject of the photograph or the photograph itself. An early compilation of such pieces was called *Extant Works and Sources*. There is also the issue of black and white and colour photographs and the differences between them. Perhaps more importantly, they all have a necessary myopia of focus, a re-iteration of the themes of his work: the lampshade armatures at sunset, the empty *abats-jours*.

We should examine more closely the development of some of his earlier work. In the early nineteen sixties, his post-cubist painting turned towards construction, and the paintings themselves became almost serial. They can historically be seen alongside more systematic works from other artists in this grouping.

By the mid-sixties, this constructive axis of his work could be confused with aspects of kineticism and the Groupe de Recherche d'Art Visuel, and his *Cubic Projections* of 1968, has indeed been much imitated. There is however always a sense of assemblage or bricolage about the work of Bill Culbert, a different legacy of Duchamp and Schwitters, always an affirmation of the balance between art and living, the 'bien-fait' of Création Permanente of Robert Filliou, a celebration of quotidian ordinariness.

3

Bill Culbert died in 2019 in the hamlet of Croagnes, Saint-Saturnin-lès-Apt, in the Vaucluse in the south of France, where he had lived and worked for the past sixty years. He was born in Port Chalmers, Dunedin, New Zealand, and came to London in 1957 to attend the Royal College of Art and study painting. He arrived by cargo ship, and due to a dockers' strike in New York during his passage, he would see *Guernica* in The Museum of Modern Art and Duchamp's *Large Glass* and *Étants Donnée* in Philadelphia.

He made his world by travelling to and living in Provence, with its relentless and revealing light. In the paintings of the early time spent there, Bill had devised his own form of late-cubism, to include the 2CV car moving through the landscape and forest, journeys and travel illuminated by its headlights.

By the mid-sixties, a more pure abstraction gave way to the machines and artifacts of light, almost simultaneous with the kinetics of the Groupe de Recherche de l'Art Visuel. But the works of Bill Culbert were always more questioning than merely perceptual, and with revelatory humour. He developed an assembly of lamps, tables, chairs, and other domestic objects picked from the refuse tips of the Luberon valley, put to work in his cluster of rebuilt houses and studios, using and making available light, and light available.

These explorations were most often photographed and with the photograph presented as the work itself. The work itself could also be the drawing of built pieces and pieces to be built, often a working inventory, with the instructions for making them. The drawings were, at times, also pure form, with the swift and spare open line begun in his earliest work, enhanced by his trusted Parker 51 fountain pen designed by Moholy-Nagy.

There was always wine, and the consequence of wine poured into a glass, the refraction, the shadow, its lucidity. *Small Glass, Pouring Light,*

Bill Culbert, Tournus, 1990.

1983, a seminal work on that subject, is now permanently installed in the Chateau d'Oiron in the Poitou region of western France.

In lean times, Bill Culbert stayed alive by teaching in many art schools, more persistently in Trent Polytechnic, Nottingham, and for many years latterly, on the MA course at Reading University. I met Bill in the heady days of conceptualism in the late nineteen sixties in Nottingham, where physical work did not abound. There was much discussion. We were both dismissed from the course in 1972, he for "fraternising with students". I was one of them.

Working with Roger Ackling

There is an aspect of the work of Roger Ackling that might easily be forgotten in its unfamiliarity. More usually, parallel lines are burnt by a lens, as closely apart as possible, onto flotsam, found perhaps from the middle of a journey. Drawing as notation of an event, a time, a place recorded. There is another genre of work however that exactly fits his sensibility and temperament, whilst at the same time suggesting a further objectification of the process of the work. This may also have led to the use of the ready-made artifacts and items of stationery in some of his later pieces. Perhaps it is an adaption of the pure drawing of the earliest work towards an openness and anticipation of the possibility of collaboration with others; there was always a suggested collectivity about his work as a teacher.

I was introduced to Roger Ackling in 1977 by Les Coleman, who had brought him along to Camberwell—at the time they were both working as gardeners in Wimbledon—and the first exhibition was made at Coracle Press in the early part of 1981. *Drawings from the Outer Hebrides*, was presented as a book of screenprinted facsimiles of the pieces themselves, with the corresponding prints placed under glass, substituted by each of the eight actual objects in their appropriate position on top of the glass. These were arranged on specially constructed display tables throughout the tall narrow space of the gallery. Indeed, the whole project was a collaboration between Roger Ackling and screen-printer and artist Martin Rogers, who had developed a continuous-tone form of reproduction, which especially suited the tonality and surface of the originals.

The second exhibition, in January 1983, was a complete departure from all the expectations of his usual work. It consisted of furniture pieces developed in collaboration by Roger Ackling with Martin Rosati, from the time he spent teaching at the London College of Furniture in Whitechapel. There was a generosity to this work, something of his listening and response to others, conducted over so many years.

In the September of that same year, there was a third exhibition at the Camberwell Coracle, *Cloud Drawings*, re-establishing the main tenet and fastidiousness of the work, and demonstrating that his drawing was possible even on the most overcast day, when the sun hides behind the clouds.

Invitation card for Roger Ackling, *Cloud Drawings*, 1983.

A History of the Airfields of Lincolnshire, anodised aluminium letters on slabs of excavated concrete runway, Skellingthorpe, Lincolnshire, 2003.

A History of the Airfields of Lincolnshire

A visit to my forgotten one-word poem (with a title of any length, as the prescription says, but this one is fixed for its subject and purpose), just outside the village of Skellingthorpe west and a bit north of Lincoln. It sits beside a long-distance cycle trial, in this section from Newark to Lincoln. It was a delight to see it renovated, re-riveted and well maintained after all these years, and how it has fallen into the grass cutting regime of the local parish.

The seven slabs of airfield concrete were taken from RAF Swinderby down the road further south, skilfully sawn and transplanted from flat to vertical in 2002. The next year, Erica and I glued on the orange anodised aluminium letters with the fiercest epoxy and a contraption that allowed it to set. But it was not strong enough for the long term, and any lone cyclist with a screwdriver could prise off a 'p' as a momento, or 'poppie' for their mantelpiece. Fortunately we lost very few, and there were a couple of spares.

Hugely physical for a poem, you might feel, but I always see it as my bit of Richard Serra, and maybe the true sensation of the poem is unchanged in its meaning by any of this?

Some Notes on 'Affinity'

Affinity (overleaf) could be seen as a homage to Ian Hamilton Finlay and the genesis of Concrete Poetry from Modernism, via a seemingly absurd parallel series of quasi-dadaistic names of boats from the Everard Shipping Fleet. F. T. Everard & Sons was started by Frederick

Affinity, 2021.

T. Everard towards the end of the nineteenth century to operate Thames Barges, and the company both built them and managed a fleet of them. Boats/ships were either named after family members or given the suffix "ity" e.g. Amity and Annuity. The one name they do not use or include is perhaps the most obvious one, 'Affinity'.

Finlay's *Ocean Stripe 5*, published by Tarasque Press in 1968, places images from *Fishing News* alongside seminal texts of the advent of modernist poetry, from Kurt Schwitters, Paul de Vree and Ernst Jandl. The collage of the invented names of the boats and the constant presence of the Everard ensign on each boat, is my offering. A quotation from a letter written by Ian Hamilton Finlay to the French spatialist poet Pierre Garnier on 17th September 1963 is adjacent in a small square frame, as a 'label' to the work. I first encountered this in *Image* magazine, Kingsland Prospect Press, London, 1964. Subsequently it has been reprinted on several other occasions, but quite recently in *A Model of Order*, edited by Thomas A. Clark (WAX366, 2009). I use the quotation, acknowledged as originating from Ian Hamilton Finlay, for the purpose of illuminating my thesis.

The photographs used as backgrounds in the work are printed digitally in black and white, with the ensign or chevron of the shipping company highlighted in red, on acid-free mould-made paper. They are printed in strips the height of the space between the shelves, so that they are exactly to position. The model boats, scaled to the size of the final work, were made by Harry Piel in Holtgast, Germany, over a period of years.

A first attempt at this work was produced at the time of *Brancusi's Sewing Box & Other Works*, an arrangement by Eiji Watanabe, Simon Cutts, Erica Van Horn, and Coracle, as part of Assembridge Nagoya 2016. Previously, a casebound book, *Affinity*, was jointly published by Coracle and Peter Foolen Editions, Eindhoven in 2011. The alphabetical sequence of black and white archival photographs of boats are ordered alphabetically by vessel, with Finlay's letter to Garnier printed in continuous excerpts beneath each image:

> I feel that the main use of theory may well be that of concentrating the attention in a certain area—of providing a context which is favourable to the actual work. I like G Vantongerloo's remark: "Things must be approached through sensitivity rather than understanding..."; this being especially acceptable from Vantongerloo since he is far from being against understanding (it seems to me)—his 'must' I take to mean 'must' because the world is such and we are so... An understanding (theoretical explanation) of concrete (in general) poetry is, for me, an attempt to find a non-concrete prose parallel to, or secular expression of, the kind of feeling, or even more basically, 'being', which says, if one listens carefully to the time, and if one is not sequestered in society, that such-and-such a mode of using words—this kind of syntax, this sort of construction—is 'honest' and 'true'... One of the Cubists—I forget who—said that it was after all difficult for them to make cubism because they did not have, as we have, the example of cubism to help them. I wonder if we are not all a little in the dark, still as to the real significance of 'concrete'... For myself I cannot derive from the poems I have written any 'method' which can be applied to the writing of the next poem; it comes back, after each poem, to a level

of 'being', to an almost physical intuition of the time, or of a form...
to which I try, with huge uncertainty, to be 'true'. Just so, 'concrete'
began for me with the extraordinary (since wholly unexpected) sense
that the syntax I had been using, the movement of language in me,
at a physical level was no longer there—so it had to be replaced with
something else, with a syntax and movement that would be true
to the new feeling (which existed only in the vaguest way, since I
had, then, no form for it...). So that I see theory as a very essential
(because we are people, and people think, or should think, or should
try to think) part of our life and art; and yet I also feel that it is a
construction, very haphazard, uncertain, and by no means as yet
to be taken as definitive. And indeed, when people come together,
for whatever purpose, the good is often a by-product... it comes
as the unexpected thing. For myself, on the question of 'naming', I
call my poems 'fauve' or 'suprematist', this to indicate their relation
to 'reality'... (and you see, one of the difficulties of theory for me
is that I find myself using a word like 'reality' while knowing that
if I was asked, "What do you mean by reality?" I would simply
answer, I don't know...). I approve of Malevich's statement, "Man
distinguished himself as a thinking being and removed himself from
the perfection of God's creation. Having left the non-thinking state,
he strives by means of his perfected objects, to be again embodied
in the perfection of the absolute, non-thinking life..." That is, this
seems to me, to describe, approximately, my own need to make
poems... though I don't know what is meant by 'God'. And it also
raises the question that, though the objects might 'make it', possibly,
into a state of perfection, the poet and painter will not. I think any
pilot-plan should distinguish, in its optimism, between what man
can construct and what he actually is. I mean, new thought does not
make a new man; in any photograph of an aircrash one can see how
terribly far man stretches—from angel to animal; and one does not
want a glittering perfection which forgets that the world is, after
all, also to be made by man into his home. I should say—however
hard I would find it to justify this in theory—that 'concrete' by its
very limitations offers a tangible image of goodness and sanity; it
is very far from the now-fashionable poetry of anguish and self...
It is a model, of order, even if set in a space which is full of doubt.
(Whereas non-concrete might be said to be set in society, rather
than space, and its 'satire', its 'revolt', are only disguised symptoms
of social dishonesty. This, I realise, goes too far; I do not mean to
say that society is 'bad'.)... I would like, if I could, to bring into
this, somewhere the unfashionable notion of 'Beauty', which I find
compelling and immediate, however theoretically inadequate. I
mean this in the simplest way—that if I was asked, 'Why do you like
concrete poetry?' I could truthfully answer 'Because it is beautiful'.

The Clustered Hang

The curator David Brown often talked about 'the thick hang' or 'the boom-boom cluster', the apogee of Victorian domestic picture-hanging that you might see in early photographs of Pre-Raphaelite parlours. As a collector of art, he always assumed that you could hang anything in a domestic interior, even minimal and conceptual works, like Richard Long's *A Line Made by Walking*, a postcard work by Gilbert and George, or Sol LeWitt's maps with shapes removed from them. At the same time he also talked of collecting only works that were A1++ (A1 double-plus). I suppose it was the domestic scale of many of the Coracle works that caught his attention. While living at Coracle Press in Camberwell in the late 1970s, he had much time to inspect them.

I was making letter-racks in different styles in the mid-seventies, and David Brown alighted on two of them replicating Monet's *Haystacks*, 1890–91, dawn and dusk, whereby you could hold your cards and letters and other paper detritus between two perspectively diminishing cut-outs in painted wood. *Homage to Seurat*, 1972, a printed and collaged folded card with cake-decorations,

Haystack Letter-rack, after Claude Monet, 1976.

'hundreds and thousands' as they have been called, sprinkled onto a rectangle of glue on its front, was often met with disdain for its coyness. When David Brown bought a framed copy for the 'Paintings in Hospitals' scheme, there was a certain reluctance to hang it, and only by his insistence was it shown at all. I suppose they felt there was little redemption for an ill patient in its seeming frivolity.

Martin-pêcheur

I think it was first suggested by Stuart Mills that we should do an exhibition with Martin Rogers in the very early days of Coracle in Camberwell, around the autumn of 1976. They were both teaching on the Foundation Course at Derby, and Stuart had seen the emerging 'Instruments for Outdoor Use' and the screen prints alongside. Stuart had asked him to make a poster for the visit of Jonathan Williams to Derby around 1974—'How to Cook A Phoenix & Other Stories'. Martin had learned a very graphic form of screenprinting at Corsham School of Art: firm line, solid ground and colours. This eventually led to a way of equivalencing physical material, like the substance of wood, in print, by a series of shifts of the printing screen to form continuous tone. Not content with just that he also began to make the objects themselves, and by 1978 or '79, we had his *Mallet Box with Four Soundboards* (shown p.129) in the doorway entrance to the shop in Camberwell New Road, to be clattered by visitors when they arrived. Amazingly it lasted many months, if not nearly a year.

Stuart Mills's poem for Gael Turnbull says quite a lot about the relationship to material from two different points of view:

> If we came together, you and I
> on a walk together,
> the tree you would take
> to put in your garden.
>
> But I would climb up with
> a sharp knife
> to cut out some wood,
> this my joy to take back.
>
> Your tree
>   growing birds
> and the children playing.
>
> My wood
>   shaped and polished
> in a corner to touch.
>
> Shade from your tree
> Touch from my wood.
> A wood full of trees
> a tree full of wood.

I remember long trips with Martin around this time. One was to fetch a van-full of handmade paper from the Moulin de Larroque in Couze-et-Saint-Front in the Dordogne, enough to do two or three editions that Coracle had begun. There were dinners, and great wine to be had, and even a few cases of a wonderful Loire Sauvignon squeezed into the van from Montmorillon. I have subsequently revisited the auberge we found there: it's not the same, but you can still get a lunch for fourteen euros.

Shortly afterwards, we made a long rambling trip to Cologne and Amsterdam, visiting bookshops, picking up books—a trip paid for by collecting Gilbert and George catalogues for their London gallery. To this day, I can see Martin sat next to a very glamorous Coosje van Bruggen and Claes Oldenburg at the huge dinner for the occasion. But the main purpose of the journey was the bookshops, the early Walther König in Cologne, Amsterdam before Boekie Woekie (if ever there was Amsterdam before BW), and just after Ulises Carrión had finished with Other Books and So as a bookshop. It was part of a sense we both had that you had to get what you made out into the world.

In 1981, he printed all the facsimile parts to be assembled for Roger Ackling's *Helping Hand* edition. Martin's 1982 exhibition in Camberwell consisted of a trellis over the entire back wall of the gallery, and its invitation card was a section of it in a cardboard envelope, sent out through the post. In front of the trellis was the huge kit for a pergola in a wooden box.

The Arts Council of England made some attempt to buy it, but then settled for a more modest, manageable work *A Set of Wooden Markers* from 1979. In 1983, Martin built the vast tunnel of wooden staves and canvas for *'Assemble Here!'* at the Puck Building in New York, and a year later, wheelbarrows of fence posts stood outside the Serpentine Gallery in Kensington Garden in *Salon d'Automne*.

It was a more fallow time in our relationship in the later eighties as I was occupied with Victoria Miro and her gallery, before deciding definitely to return to the singularity of publishing in the early nineties. I think Martin was on a similar course of returning to base, and by 1991 he began to form the Research Group for Artist Publications from his department at the University of Derby. I believe unconsciously he began to give up his individual work for the idea of a collective one, and the first collaborative projects ensued from there. The conferences, the annexing of money from the European Union funds, the disastrous *Mail Art Project* of 1996, where cheeky exchange students from France and Spain sent far too cryptic comments to aficionados in the field. These were also the years of Frankfurt Book Fair with the work of the Research Group as the stand next to Coracle.

Martin came and helped me with my own house in Ireland laying floors and roofing, and a little later building the bread oven which we seem to use only for smoking these days. Even last year he built a small wall there.

Important books of these years included the critical study of the work our great friend Brian Lane, *The Printed Performance*, and *Repetivity: Platforms and Approaches for Publishing*, where the title says

Martin Rogers, *Mallet Box with Four Soundboards*, 1978.

it all. But the great Research Group project he began was The Small Publishers Fair in November 2002, which for that year was held in the Festival Hall on the South Bank. The following year it moved to the Conway Hall in Red Lion Square, the shrine of Bloomsbury Humanism, former home of the Anarchists Bookfair, with "To Thine Own Self Be True" painted on the proscenium arch portico. It has been there every year this past decade, and must continue there as long as it can. It is his legacy, as much as the attempt to move the Research Group archive library and papers to the Site Gallery in Sheffield, with whom he had a long association. A Sol LeWitt wall drawing with an almost complete exhibition of his books, and a conference of the work, took place there in 2010. The archive of the Research Group there could become an expanding centre for further activity surrounding small press publishing, and a resource for documentation of the field.

Martin had an intriguing way of cleaning his knife at the breakfast table that I had never seen before. He would insert the blade into the thickness of a slice of bread on its cut edge to clean it, between using the butter dish and the jar of marmalade, and thereby not carrying one to the other. It was part of his measuredness, his respect for the tools for the job. This ran alongside a boyish openness, bordering on an optimism. He would listen to ideas and let them happen as far as they could. It was a rather fuss-less process, without fretting at that point. If it worked, it worked, and if not it probably just fell away. This became more and more important an attitude to receiving possibilities for books to be done by the Research Group, and indeed, the first posthumous book is called *On Listening*.

There was always a sense of display, of presented-ness, about his working space, a projection of his openness for others to enquire into, to see what was being done and considered, a sense of teaching. And just as there was always a sense of potential music about the objects themselves he began by making, so there was about the more composite projects—*Acoustic Shadow* done for Site Gallery, and *Domestic Acoustic* made for the Stuttgart Kunstverein. More recently we had talked about a Symphony for Six Adana printing machines, which might have been done at Site Gallery at the time of Print It, if he'd not been taken ill.

The Cagean sense of music is one of continuousness: music only stops when we turn away and stop listening. As John Cage himself said "there will never be silence till death comes, which never comes."

bagatelles

1

trellis &
treillage

making
a shelter

of foliage

2

trestle
& trellis

making
a framework

of lattice

The Pencils of Matsutani

There is always the process of days spent in the studio, which may also be office, library, kitchen and archive, from where Takesada Matsutani writes and sends handwritten letters every day, and records the addresses in meticulously structured lists—a remarkably literary and domestic activity for so abstract an artist.

It is not only the work itself, but the resoluteness of a life, in which nothing is thrown away, like the ten years of shavings from pencils all sharpened with a knife, held in one bucket. At the same time, elsewhere on shelves, around the studio and on his desk, you will find all the staples he has ever taken out of canvases, the ends of crayons that are now too short to hold.

Across from the studio is a wooden box maker who has many standard sizes of small boxes with brass hinges and clasps for the fastening of the lid, but also long narrow boxes with sliding lids. Our task was to choose the right box to make an edition, with the whole quantity of pencil shavings divided to fill each box, the contents thus determining the size of the edition, and also suggesting some sort of measure of his life in Paris. The edition and its title contain an absence, and all we are left with are the remains.

We finally divided up the 6B pencil shavings of Takesada Matsutani in small bundles of cellophane bags, with a label fastened with twisted wire to seal them. The labels were rubber stamped with the narrative of

Takesada Matsutani, *The Pencils of Matsutani*, edition of forty-three. Assembled in an open production on 9th March 2016 at Librairie Yvon Lambert, 108 rue Vieille du Temple, Paris 3.

the making of the edition and the particular number within it. We had to move sideways and put the parts into bags because not all the boxes had arrived in time. Nonetheless this made for another part in the ritual of its production, and something for the small audience of onlookers to see and puzzle over, just round the corner in a bookshop in rue Vieille du Temple. We wore white coats with project badges on the lapel pocket while we were putting the parts together, to add to the procedure of it all, and Matsutani wrote his name in calligraphy with brush and ink, under the number on the inside of the lid.

Pangaea

Yoko Terauchi arrived from Japan the other day, and in her luggage was the sculpture she made last year called *Pangaea*. It is made of two sheets of paper, each twenty-four centimetres square. They are both marked at the edge with a coloured pentel pen. One is placed on the wall, and the other is wet and formed into a sphere about the size of a ping-pong ball by being squeezed and tightened in cling-film, then left to dry completely.

Yoko Terauchi, *Pangaea*, 2017.

This descriptive mundanity of the work of course completely detracts from its purity, and it is one of the most purely abstract things I have seen. It is a serial work, in as much as there are several colours in the pentel range that she will use to make the work, perhaps as many as twenty.

Because of its simplicity and scale, it is quite difficult to know where the work belongs. Certainly the 'gallery' might be too demonstrative, the display too gestural, which is how I have come to think of such places in recent times. And my fear is that the world is too busy to see things of such accomplished simplicity, too noisy for reductive thinking.

Well done, Yoko: it stays in the mind, and to paraphrase Sol LeWitt, once you have understood a work, a proposition, you own it. And Bertolt Brecht, I think, said that everything belongs to the one who is best for it.

Starting from Home

It is one of the delights of living where we do at this time of year in the Marais, in this city of Paris, that you can just slip out for ten minutes to see something, pick up something, and return to the eyrie, without preparation. No long train journeys with coats and bags, no rest stop.

It was one such jaunt that took us to a gallery round the corner in rue Sainte-Anastase. I knew Peter Downsbrough was in town making an exhibition, and thought we should say hello. Especially in the light of a book we thought to do of his photographs of Cork City.

Contrary to any reservation about the current state of galleries, or maybe because of it, his installation was pure delight. It's a precarious balance to have just enough to hold the eye and mind. Peter is one of those artists whose work has intensified and become even better as he's become older, more spare and precise, and with a clearer reading of any space he is given. I am always amazed at the simplicity of devices in the construction of his work, the home-madeness that leads to such an abstraction and austerity of the finished work. With Peter Downsbrough, the black-painted wooden dowel rods hang from small painted nails, hooks and eyes on the wall and ceiling. The vinyl sign is cut and divided and positioned with such care and judgement of its space.

Fred Sandback, another artist of the space of a room, stretched coloured rayon yarn bought at the haberdashers from wall to floor and ceiling, fixed by small ferules of brass tube he drills into the surface. They both divide space in a sublime and yet totally understandable way.

Both of them seem almost the last of a generation of Americans who come with a particularly incisive development from a starting place. I am thinking of Hugh Kenner's *A Homemade World* of the modernist writers, re-applied here. It is something that continues through the simplicity of means of their work to the completeness of its abstraction. You can read it in their most understated, seemingly empty work.

It is the organisational ability of a generation of conceptual, post-visual artists, mostly American, that distinguishes them. They have built new worlds not conceived of before. But it is their office structures that bear and sustain it, really a form of warehousing and storage, packaging in a physical sense, for a systematic presentation, a catalogue or manual of parts that could be called on when needed to be installed, an office for its organisation.

These artists were not working in any intellectually existing continuum, but with a new consistency that had to be invented. They were like workmen from more vernacular geographic parts, doing a daily job, making their office and workshop, far from the artiness of the so-called 'studio', and its later excrescence, the artist of fame.

Notes on the work of Sol LeWitt

> "I can only say that the gallery as it is constituted in our time has the obligation to show the art of the time. I am more interested in artists' books which contain art ideas that can be had by anyone at the cost of a couple of movies. Art really cannot be bought and sold but only understood. Books do this best. The gallery is best as a publisher"—Sol LeWitt

In 1968, Sol LeWitt made a rather enigmatic work entitled *Buried Cube Containing an Object of Importance but of Little Value*. It was the period between the initial physical Cube Structures and the beginning of the Wall Drawings, which he continued for the rest of his life. In a paragraph accompanying the work, he cites Gertrude Stein who said that a work of art is either priceless or worthless, and he brings a new generativeness, a new openness to the work made by artists. At the same time, it displaces the pejorative hierarchy of forms from the most physical to the most ephemeral. Like the ephemerality of the Wall Drawings, it changes classification.

It is within this openness, this revision of possibilities of the time, that I want to look at the implications for The Gallery as Publisher, and by extension, to The Gallery as Format, the gallery almost as a device of publication, of editorial, of grouping, of serial presentation. This will be done from samplings of Coracle activity over the years, mainly in the intermediate period of the nineteen eighties. It may not necessarily follow the schematic, serial approach of Sol LeWitt, but it is one view of some of the practical implications and pointers from his work. In this way it might even be the opposite of his conceptualism, about which he said: "The serial artist does not attempt to produce a beautiful or mysterious object, but functions merely as a clerk cataloguing the results of the premise."

For Sol LeWitt, the book was the equivalent of a larger spatial setting for the work. He said that walls were public and large and that books are small and private, and that they could both give the same information. This may well be true for his procedural way of working, but not always for the role of the book in different contexts. The book could be almost an alternative catalogue.

The understanding and making of the edition can change the content of the work. By the use of schematic limitation and reduction to the process of the printed work, the work changes from its initial conception.

Schematic and Structured Work in Other Contexts

There has always been Concrete Poetry to sanction the use of wall space for the construction of the poem, but the American conceptualists of the late nineteen sixties, especially LeWitt and the implications of his way of working, may have provided another impetus to the presented work. A new lineality, a new literalness of syntax from a different methodology of procedure; no longer only the formality of a European gestalt.

Finally, I want to return to the dichotomy of public and private that Sol LeWitt inferred in his earlier statement about walls and books, and in his 1968 work *Buried Cube*. His procedures and way of working make redundant the current performative hyper-display of the gallery: it is just a place to work in a temporary setting. As this simple role for the gallery may have been replaced by the fetishisation of its function, at the same time the new digital mediation might also have confused the platform for publishing. This, however, leaves it in an even more privileged position, to be discovered. Sol LeWitt's openness and generosity allowed for another way of working, a more casual encounter, a slower interaction, a discovery gained.

The Material Language of Carl Andre

We just caught the travelling Carl Andre history at the Musée d'Art Moderne de Paris, and it was a good time to think about his so-called 'poems', largely from earlier times in the work. I think it's a bit of a misnomer to call them that. They are really inventories of language as yet another elemental material, to be stacked, repeated, laid flat, pushed up against the wall. They use none of the devices of the language of poetry, title and play of content, metaphor as displacement and alternation, but they merely state themselves as material fact. Nothing wrong with that, I would add.

Maybe all this is too retrospective an analysis, far too formal, and they really occurred in a more spontaneous time, along with other surprising vestiges of mail art, a plethora of postcards sent to friends through the available system at your doorstep. But what I really admire now about Carl Andre is the fact that he stopped working at a given point, and resorted to the hand-held manipulations of material shapes and forms that he continues to give to friends. Not for him to become the factory of the artworld, the manufacturer of storable property and space-fillers for over-sized collections. He remains fluid and adaptable, in spite of what at first might seem a puritan monolith of chaste material.

Drinking Sculpture

Stepping out, or more like hobbling-out for the first time with a torn ankle, to see the wonderful Alighiero Boetti exhibition I had seen in London last November. There I heard that Jannis Kounellis, one of his working compatriots, had just died. The work was not close at all, but they shared a time of radical change to raw materials that we have still never recovered from. Hearing of him in that context caused a reverie of one of his great works that I had seen in the early nineties in the middle of France, in the most unlikely of venues.

It was in Chagny, Burgundy that Pietro Sparta made a gallery to show his Arte Povera friends and a few others, largely, if I remember, because of the presence in Chagny of the truly great restaurant Maison Lameloise. Because the artists wanted to eat there, they could be persuaded to come to the middle of nowhere and make a large exhibition. Pietro Sparta had a partner in the gallery who was called Pascale Petite. There is a poet in Britain of nearly the same name, and I have never known if she took another career. There was loose talk at the time of Pietro doing a show with Ian Hamilton Finlay, if I remember correctly. Not a bad idea I thought to myself, since their combined names made Little Sparta, the homestead of Mr Finlay!

Passing through Chagny on the way south one day, Erica and I encountered the remarkable 1988 work of Kounellis, made of glasses of grappa and cut lead shapes. I understood there to be as many as forty thousand glasses of grappa, and the work was arranged in a far more fugitive state than the more formalistic museum presentation of future years. The smell was overwhelming, and you could hardly enter the rooms containing the work. Of course, the grappa evaporated and had to be topped-up continuously. It makes an interesting aside to the Bill Culbert work *Small Glass Pouring Light* (shown p.115), now in the Chateau d'Oiron in France, which is conserved by drinking its contents, in this case red wine. But socially involving as both pieces might be, here there was just far too much grappa for drinking as a means of conservation. They are both great works and live in the memory. They are far from the party-pieces of Gilbert and George, formally titled *Drinking Sculptures* as such, and presented as the near-diaristic narrative of the performance of a pub-crawl, the remains of which are the snap photographs framed in the funereal black edges of passepartout.

The Vertical Earth Kilometer

It was saddening to hear last month of the end of Walter De Maria. He was visiting his hundred-year-old mother in California, he being a mere stripling of seventy seven. He was the most quizzical of artists, arriving from the world of bands in which he was the drummer, the New York of the mid-sixties, the neo-fluxus world of happenings.

He has left us with at least four major enigmas, that remain utterly fresh to the imagination every time you consider them. Thanks to the Dia Art Foundation they are maintained, where they need to be, and can be visited, at varying degrees of inconvenience, at any time. *The Broken Kilometer* still glistens from the ground floor of an industrial building in West Broadway, New York, and *The Earth Room* is still warm and humid in Wooster Street. *The Lightning Field* is a little more tricky in the desert of New Mexico, but it can be done as a pilgrimage.

But the piece that fascinates me perhaps the most is *The Vertical Earth Kilometer* in Kassel, Germany, made in 1979. You are asked to believe that the round brass plate, set in a square of sandstone, descends a whole kilometre into the earth. It is a structure of belief, as is the notion that fronds of lightning will play in their designated field in New Mexico. Walter De Maria's work indeed seems to resound with the idea of belief, as the proposition of conceptualism, and he is perhaps its main proponent. They are sort of Catholic works. We have to believe in Walter Da Maria's proposition, just as we have to believe in, say, the detail of time and geography of a work by Richard Long, before we can move to the next step.

Unique Forms of Continuity in Space

The 1913 sculpture *Unique Forms of Continuity in Space* by the Futurist Umberto Boccioni has a varied genesis. The original work was in plaster, and was never cast into bronze in his lifetime. His original plaster is displayed at the Museu de Arte Contemporânea da Universidade de São Paulo. Two bronze casts were made in 1931, one of which is displayed at the Museum of Modern Art in Manhattan. Two more were made in 1949, one of which is displayed at the Metropolitan Museum of Art in New York, and other at the Museum of 20th Century in Milan. Two also were made in 1972, one of which is displayed at the Tate Modern in London. Another eight were made in 1972, not from the plaster original, but from one of the 1949 bronze casts. One of these bronze casts is in the Kröller-Müller Museum in Otterlo, Netherlands. In 2014, a bronze was donated to the National Gallery of Cosenza. It is fitting too that the work graces the reverse of the Italian twenty cent coin of the euro currency, and this we might celebrate in this sequence of things.

It was clearly most influenced by *The Winged Victory of Samothrace*, also called the Nike of Samothrace, a marble Hellenistic sculpture of Nike, the Greek goddess of victory, created in the second century BC. Since 1884, it has been prominently displayed in the Louvre and is one of a small number of major Hellenistic statues surviving in the original, rather than as a Roman copy. The *Victory* soon became a cultural icon, to which artists responded in many different ways. When Filippo Tommaso Marinetti issued his Futurist Manifesto in 1909, he chose to contrast his movement with the seemingly defunct artistic sentiments of the *Winged Victory*: "a racing car, rushing over explosives, is more beautiful than *The Winged Victory of Samothrace*."

Boccioni's sculpture in turn borrows from that Hellenistic sculpture of Nike. It is also perhaps in the same vein that the images of split hot water bottles with burgeoning plaster insets by Maud Cotter, work in parallel to the products of a sports and shoe company named

Maud Cotter, *Unique Form of Continuity in Space*, 2018–19.

after the Greek goddess herself. In the manner of such stylistically improbable pairings initiated by the futurists with their manifesto, why not also with a hot-water bottle, which in turn to this day, is still called Mezzo Marito in Italy—the half-husband, becoming pillows and purses.

Wartesaal

Reinhard Mucha, *Wartesaal*, 1979–1982, Galerie Max Hetzler, 1982.

I'm rarely in Paris without remembering Reinhard Mucha's *Wartesaal*, seen at Centre Pompidou in 1986, in what was the big open space just off the corner of Rue du Renard. There were several very large cumulative works in his retrospective of the time, stacked furniture, ladders, dissemblies of rooms, re-makes. But the one piece that really struck me, an entire room in itself, was the 'Waiting Room' which Mucha built in Düsseldorf between 1979 and 1982, and modified in 1986 for this exhibition.

It is made of a system of stacks of drawers in what look like dexion supports, butted and bolted together, intersecting at right angles, and incorporating a cumbersome gothic wardrobe. This in itself gives the whole installation placement, and is the sort of accoutrement you might find in any isolated railway station across the network. At the same time it anchors the piece from being completely self-enclosed, and gives it its veiled narrative. There are eleven of these wheeled shelving units, each with twenty-two drawers. In each drawer is the name of a station in Germany, painted on boards, each of them of six letters, 242 place-names in total, taken from a 1948 freight directory first published in 1943. They are rendered in the modernist type of the German rail system. Because of the need to open the drawers, you are passively invited to examine and move name-plates to a lit table in the middle of the piece, and in the hue of the fluorescent strips running at the top of each unit and the top of the wardrobe.

Reinhard Mucha, *Wartesaal, 1979–1982*, Galerie Max Hetzler, 1982.

In its nostalgia, its soulfulness, *Wartesaal* embodies the whole journey of Europe, even if taken from one particular place, almost as a cross-section of it. It also begins to use the materials of Reinhard Mucha's construction in a more abstract, less narrative way, and forms the basis of much of his later work in which these place-names continue to be used.

It might seem like a fragile remit for this piece, but it is as present for me as the Eiffel Tower. Even if it has not existed there for thirty years, whenever I turn that corner from Rue du Renard into Place Beaubourg, I am amongst it.

Coracle Bibliography 1975–2022

* In association with other publishers
** Victoria Miro Gallery
*** workfortheeyetodo

1975

A Book of Braids
Simon Cutts, Kay Roberts

Leafmould
Simon Cutts, Karl Torok

Transit of Venus
David Willetts

Treacle Sandwich Flagpole
Simon Cutts

Mr G White of Messrs Green & White
Simon Cutts

Poinsettia
Simon Cutts

The Embroidered Topiary
Simon Cutts

The Weatherhouse and other works
Exhibition catalogue

A Coracle 1–12
Broadsheet

1976

Good Hoofs
Stephen Duncalf

Garden of the Anterior
Bernard Lassus

Hedgerow Airport
Stuart Mills

1977

Paintings 1972–76
David Willetts

Tunnel
Stephen Duncalf

Miniatures
Exhibition catalogue

The Topiarist 3
Simon Cutts

A Letterwrack for an Old Pal
Simon Cutts

Twice
Stuart Mills, Laurie Clark

Tips
Stephen Duncalf

Christmas Apples
Stuart Mills, David Willetts

On Time!
Stephen Duncalf

Huts, By-ways, Engines, Orchard
Stephen Duncalf

Paintings shown at Coracle Press and the Ibis Gallery during 1977
David Prentice

Inside-Outside
Daryl Viner

Artist's Blocks
Exhibition catalogue

The Dustcover
Stephen Duncalf

1978	1979	1980
Twelve Pieces Richard Wilson	*Aggie Weston's No.14* Thomas Meyer	*Wind Instruments* Richard Wilson
February Les Coleman	*Waddington's* Simon Cutts	*It is so green outside it is difficult to leave the window* Shelagh Wakely
fo(u)ndlings Exhibition catalogue	*Instruments for Outdoor Use* Martin Rogers	
Monotones Simon Cutts	*Green Gauge* Martin Fidler	*Pins* Simon Cutts
Analytical Dottiness Trevor Winkfield	*Portrait Photographs* Jonathan Williams	*Some Principals and Practice of Twelve Modern Art Styles* Gerry Hunt
Sources and Structure in Painting and Drawing David Prentice	*Poinsettia 3* Simon Cutts	*Print: book and object* Simon Cutts
City Gardens Stephen Duncalf	*Professsor Thomas Bodkin and Cezanne* Stuart Mills, Stephen Duncalf	*A Walk Past Standing Stones* * Richard Long
Coracle Press in Amsterdam Exhibition catalogue	*Moschatel Press* Exhibition catalogue	*'on loan'* Exhibition catalogue
	A Ruskin Sketchbook Thomas A. Clark	*Winter Fruit* Simon Cutts
	Blossoms and Flowers Leonard McComb	*Un Air Rosé* Bernard Lassus
	Aggie Weston's No.15 John Blakemore	
	Aggie Weston's No.16 Richard Long	
	New Paintings Martin Fidler	

1981

Twelve Works
Richard Long

Kinds of Clouds
Les Coleman

PG Tips
Simon Cutts

Caravanserai
Simon Cutts

Pails of Weather
Simon Cutts, Stuart Mills

A Selection of English Books for the Frankfurter Kunstverein
Simon Cutts

Feuilles Albumesques
Simon Cutts

wind motet
Simon Cutts

The Objecting Word
Gavin Bennett

The Little Red Library of Little Red Books
Peter Bailey

Aggie Weston's No.17
Review

4 Years at Coracle Press
Exhibition catalogue

Helping Hand
Roger Ackling

1982

South Bank Show
Exhibition catalogue

a fold of sewn cotton
Simon Cutts

The Economies
John Bevis

Song of the Skylark *
Hamish Fulton

The Delian Seasons
Jonathan Williams, Karl Torok

Sappho
Thomas Meyer, Sandra Fisher

odéon oceàn
Simon Cutts

Cha Cha Cha
Stephen Willats

New Work made at Coracle Press
Exhibition catalogue

Book Workshop 82-83
Coracle Press

Trellis
Martin Rogers

Abats-jours
Simon Cutts

1983

Sisters of Menon *
Susan Hiller

Dry-point Reliefs 1980-82 *
Oleg Kudryashov

Tongue & Groove
Exhibition catalogue

Horizon to Horizon *
Hamish Fulton

Gnomery
Simon Cutts

Schaufelbagger und Muldenkipper
Exhibition catalogue

Les Pins
Bernard Lassus

The Landscape Approach of Bernard Lassus
Stephen Bann

Medicine Wheel
Chris Drury

Paintings 1973-83 *
Peter Joseph

Assemble Here!
Exhibition catalogue

Twilight Horizons *
Hamish Fulton

The Coracle in Docking
Invitation brochure

1984

A Year in Camberwell
Yoko Terauchi

Nineteen Eighty Four *
Exhibition catalogue

Restless *
David Tremlett

Antony Gormley *
Lynne Cooke

Sixteen Works *
Richard Long

Footnotes to a Manual of Shaker Furniture
Simon Cutts

Video Times *
Kevin Atherton

Intervention and Audience
Stephen Willats

Repeat
Exhibition Catalogue

Salon d'Automne *
Exhibition catalogue

Terra
Yoko Terauchi

Extant Work and Sources 1973-84
Bill Culbert

Mud Hand Prints
Richard Long

Low-Tech
Exhibition catalogue

The Foliage Society
John Bevis

as and of
Colin Sackett

with and within
Colin Sackett

Mr G White of Messrs Green & White
Simon Cutts

mirroirs
Simon Cutts

Weathered II *
John Cage

1985

Two Works by Paul Lincoln
Exhibition catalogue

In Tribute to Madame de Pompadour
Paul Lincoln

Plasticine work
Colin Sackett

Sappho, second edition
Sandra Fisher

Texts
Heinz Gappmayr

Triangles and Two Pinwheels *
Richard Tuttle

Evidence
Andy Goldsworthy

La Main Vert
Bernard Lassus

Landscape
Tony Cragg

Coast to Coast Walks
Hamish Fulton

Three Artists From France *
Stephen Bann, et al

1986

Sculpture 1981-86 *
Tony Hayward

Paper & Wire & Lead *
Yoko Terauchi

To Unfold
Verdi Yahooda

Selected Works 1968-1986 *
Bill Culbert

The Artist Publisher: A Survey by Coracle Press *
Exhibition catalogue

New Poems 1962/1985 *
Robert Lax

Intervention and Audience
Stephen Willats

petits airs for Margot
Simon Cutts

Homage to Homage to Seurat
Simon Cutts

Africa Footprints *
Richard Long

A twit on the painter Julian Schnabel
Helmuth Rieck

Foto-Cliché **
Exhibition catalogue

1987

The Unpainted Landscape *
Simon Cutts, et al

Sonnets and Tableaux
Sandra Fisher, Thomas Meyer

Loophole **
Richard Tuttle, Simon Cutts

Homage to Ian Hamilton Finlay **
Yves Abrioux

1988

Ebb & Flow
Yoko Terauchi

Utopiary
Simon Cutts, Karl Torok

Chewing-Gum et Spaghetti
Simon Cutts

Coracle Press Archive List 1975–1987
Catalogue

1989

Green Road **
Hamish Fulton

Drancy **
Anne Atik, R. B. Kitaj

Black Bob
Colin Sackett

Nine Poems
Simon Cutts

Palpa
Simon Cutts

Catgut and Blossom: Jonathan Williams in England
Edited David Annwn

The Coracle: Coracle Press Gallery 1975–1987
Exhibition catalogue

Bottle Combinations *
Bill Culbert

Abstraction and Empathy, Little Critic No.1 **
Thomas Bernstein, Richard Venlet

Rock Fall Echo Dust *
Hamish Fulton

A New Seed Catalogue
Simon Cutts

1990

A History of the Airfields of Lincolnshire
Simon Cutts

lines of thin pale blue and red *
Simon Cutts, Ian Hamilton Finlay

Less
Colin Sackett

Copy
Colin Sackett

Stairwell
Stephen Willats

187 Interjections from the second half of the talk by Dennis Adams
Erica Van Horn

Jewels I Have Loved
Erica Van Horn

Sans Signaux
Erica Van Horn, Simon Cutts

Disposal Bag, Italian Lessons Nos. 2 & 3
Erica Van Horn

Italian Lesson No.4
Erica Van Horn

New York Hot, New York Cold **
Paul Etienne Lincoln

Le Havre *
Bill Culbert

1989, Little Critic No.2 **
Review

Paintings 1990, Little Critic No.3 **
Kay Rosen

Eight Words from a reading at Brooklyn College
Richard Tuttle

Two chairs, two benches and a table **
Richard Tuttle

Printed Works: Ian Hamilton Finlay **
Exhibition catalogue

1991

Ducts & Tracts: Notebooks 1974–86
Stephen Duncalf

Le Jardin Des Tuileries
Bernard Lassus

The Sea is Silent: Corrected Poems 1969–1989
Stuart Mills

1989
Erica Van Horn

Argo, Italian Lesson No.6
Erica Van Horn

A brief visual inventory of the furniture and objects at Via Perseto 9
Erica Van Horn

Immortality and Freedom, Little Critic No.4
Márton Koppány

Direct from Nature, Little Critic No.5
John Bevis

Utility building, Little Critic No.6
Ulrich Rückriem

Olympe
Marie Bourget

A Van Horn Family Motto
Simon Cutts

1992

Approximate Increments
David Bellingham

Some Notes on Writing & Drinking
Bill Culbert, Simon Cutts

IHF
Simon Cutts

inkwell & paperweight
Simon Cutts

Copy, revised edition
Colin Sackett

Wirelesslessness
Colin Sackett

Cuckoo
Yoko Terauchi

Aglio 6 Olio
Simon Cutts, Erica Van Horn

Antwerp Airport
Erica Van Horn

Companions & Menus
Simon Cutts, Erica Van Horn

Spring Staircase
Simon Cutts

Patchwork, Little Critic No.7
Pip Culbert

A Country Museum, Little Critic No.8

Hypothèses pour une troisième nature
Bernard Lassus

Public Space in a Private Time *
Vito Acconci

1993

Namenlosen
Simon Cutts, Colin Sackett

The Rubber-Stamp Mini-Printer Series 1
Simon Cutts

The Translated Latrine Inscriptions of the Palazzo Davanzani
Simon Cutts

Two Views
Simon Cutts

New York High, New York Low
Paul Lincoln

Workplace 1991–1993
Don Prince

noiselesson ***
Colin Sackett

Boy Bell's Book of Envelope Interiors
Erica Van Horn

Stiles & The Pennine Way
Erica Van Horn

Water of Recess
Erica Van Horn, Simon Cutts

Lieu 1, Little Critic No.9
Bernard Lassus

Beyond Reading, Little Critic No.10
Simon Cutts

A harbour of books cards and prints: Ian Hamilton Finlay ***
Catalogue

A Windowsill of Books on Landscape
Catalogue

Cakes First *
Tessa Falvey

1994

Some Notes on Drinking & Driving
Bill Culbert, Simon Cutts

Andy Making Holes
Simon Cutts

The Waterfalls of New Hampshire in Winter
Simon Cutts

Beyond Borders
Don Prince

coil / join
Yoko Terauch

Envelope Interiors, second edition
Erica Van Horn

Identificazione
Erica Van Horn

Scraps of an Aborted Collaboration, Italian Lesson No.13
Erica Van Horn

Envelope Interiors, third edition
Erica Van Horn

Views from the Windy House *
Rob Smith

Forty Fungi
Harry Gilonis, Erica Van Horn

Envelope Interior Pin-Up Calendar 1995
Erica Van Horn

Interaction and Overlap: from the Little Magazine & Small Press Collection at University College London ***
Geoffrey Soar, David Miller

Some Implications of Poetry ***
John Janssen

Coracle at the Irish Museum of Modern Art *
Invitation

For the Voice ***
Stephen Bury

1995

An A-Z of Bird Song
John Bevis

an ode for the recovery of an olympia splendid 66
Simon Cutts

The Rubber-Stamp Mini-printer Series 2
Simon Cutts

The Landscape Approach of Bernard Lassus: 2
Stephen Bann

Docking Competitions 1991–95
Erica Van Horn, Laurie Clark

Bicycle plaque
Mark Pawson

Forever Multiples ***
Catalogue

A Selection of New Books from America and Europe ***
Catalogue

1996

lines from walls 1989–95
Simon Cutts

A Handful of Stones
Thomas Joshua Cooper

single: Words for Ian Hamilton Finlay
Various

Gumigas Zimogs: A World Guide to Rubber Stamps
Erica Van Horn

after Frank O'Hara and Morton Feldman
Simon Cutts, Erica Van Horn

Spines & Spirals: The Norfolk Books 1990–96
Exhibition catalogue

Damaged Nature, Auto-Destructive Art
Gustav Metzger

Envelope Interior Pin-Up Calendar 1997
Erica Van Horn

Five Prints
Tony Cragg

Some Alternatives to the White Cube, Little Critic No.11
Thomas A. Clark

Coracle Postcards 1978–1996
Boxed set

1997

An Envelope Interior Art History
Erica Van Horn, Harry Gilonis

The A. Goldsworthy Questionnaires
Simon Cutts

The View from the Horizon
Tim Robinson

Fauve Construction
Simon Cutts, Erica Van Horn

Moschatel Press 1973–1966 ***
Catalogue

1998

Double Clutch Two Block Walk, Carpe Diem II *
Richard Nonas

8 Cities: Temple Bar International Print Show 1998 *

Five Poems, Little Critic No.12
Hamish Maclaren

A Ventile for Tullio
Simon Cutts, Erica Van Horn

The Space of the Page *
Catalogue

translucent imperfectly transparent, glass edition
Simon Cutts

1999

anyone
Simon Cutts

Cafe Alt Wien
Simon Cutts

Some Memorials: The Photo-diaries
Mick Williamson

14 Blackthorns
Erica Van Horn, Simon Cutts

15 Blackthorns
Erica Van Horn

The Pig Poems
Spike Hawkins, Erica Van Horn

Only Paranoics Survive, Carpe Diem III *
Peter Weibel

2000

A Smell of Printing: Poems 1988–1999 *
Simon Cutts

A Prime for the Millennium *
John B. Cosgrave

Letterpress: Tony Zwicker 1925–2000
Erica Van Horn, Simon Cutts

A History of the Airfields of Lincolnshire II
Simon Cutts

A History of the Airfields of Lincolnshire: a proposal for the installation of the poem
Simon Cutts

Ex Libris: John Janssen at Sixty
Various

Repetivity: Platforms and approaches to publishing *
Exhibition catalogue

The Presence of Landscape: Printed Objects, Cards & Books, Coracle Press 1975–2000 *
Exhibition catalogue

Water of Recess
Erica Van Horn, Simon Cutts

2001

Necklace of Tongues
Alice Maher

I Build My Time: Columns, Grottos, Niches
Klaus Stadtmueller

The Printed Performance: Brian Lane Works 1966–99 *
Edited by Martin Rogers & Simon Cutts

Olwen Fouere in the Bull's Wall, Little Critic No.13
Tim Robinson

Eight Poems, Little Critic No.14
Clere Parsons

Little Books & Other Little Publications, Little Critic No.15
Anne Moeglin-Delcroix

2002

The Money Jar
Erica Van Horn, Simon Cutts

Fredson Bowers and the Irish Wolfhound
J. C. C. Mays

Some Words for Living Locally
Erica Van Horn

Airmail Envelope Interiors
Erica Van Horn, Simon Cutts

Nearing Arcueil *
Erica Van Horn, Simon Cutts

Kidnapped
Susan Howe

Bedhangings II
Susan Howe

Poems for my Shorthand Typist
Stuart Mills

For it not to be worth the paper it is printed on it has to be printed, Little Critic No.16
Les Coleman

2003

Of Colour In Craft *
Brian Kennedy

Notional: Field Notes
Katie Holten

A Canticle for Fred Sandback
Simon Cutts

A Phylum Press Selection, Little Critic No.17
Edited by Richard Deming, Nancy Kuh

The Vegetable Plot at L8511
Tim Robinson

Envelope Interior Pin-Up Calendar 2004
Erica Van Horn

2004

Englshpublshing: Writing and readings 1991–2002 *
Colin Sackett

Boats, Cots, Punts & Wherries: The Notebooks of Thomas Cuddihy
Shay Hurley

Rusted
Erica Van Horn

An English Dictionary of French Place Names
Simon Cutts

eclogues
Simon Cutts

sourcebook
Simon Cutts

Two Peelings, 1993 & 2004
Erica Van Horn

MiMo: A story
Erica Van Horn

2005

oeillets des poètes
Simon Cutts

Tin funnel, jug & dish
Erica Van Horn, Simon Cutts

Lemon Red
Cralan Kelder

The Purification of Fagus Sylvatica Var Pendula
Paul Etienne Lincoln

New Potatoes
Helen O'Leary, Paul Chidester

Forty Shades of Green *
Brian Kennedy, Simon Cutts, Erica Van Horn

Vinyl: Project for installation
Exhibition catalogue

with yellow pears
Simon Cutts

Our friend Sid
Erica Van Horn, Simon Cutts

2006

Led Astray By Language
Jonathan Williams, Thomas Meyer, Nancy Kuhl, Richard Deming, Erica Van Horn, Simon Cutts

With My Left Hand
Erica Van Horn

Stoppage
Erica Van Horn

A Little Book of Cockles
Carla Phillips, Laurie Clark

Certain Trees *
Exhibition catalogue

Folded Napkins
Erica Van Horn

N11: A Musing, Little Critic No.18
J. C. C. Mays

Numbers
Maurice Scully

Rue Montorgueil Decked out with Flags, glass edition
Simon Cutts

2007

French Pastry
Cralan Kelder

peuran / pears
Harry Gilonis

Gifts from the Government, Living Locally No.11
Erica Van Horn

Small Houses: The Buildings of Tom Browne
Erica Van Horn

A Few Cups
Erica Van Horn

A little bit of butter *
Peter Foynes

as if it is at all: Some Poems 1995–2006 *
Simon Cutts

Some Forms of Availability: Critical Passages on the Book and Publishing *
Simon Cutts

A Canticle for Fred Sandback
Simon Cutts

the only function of the envelope interior, Little Critic No.19
Erica Van Horn

Saffron, glass edition *
Simon Cutts

2008

Driven-Out, Ditched & Deserted
Jason Clark

Forty Funghi, second edition
Harry Gilonis, Erica Van Horn

An Album of Interiors
Erica Van Horn

Black Bob, second edition
Colin Sackett

short-cuts
Erica Van Horn, Simon Cutts

Avenue Crescent: The Rain Paintings 2005–2008
Stephen Skidmore

8 Old Irish apples, Living Locally No.13
Erica Van Horn, Simon Cutts

Some Alternatives to Flock
John Bevis

Made in English: The Collected Poems
Stuart Mills

The Triumphal Processsion of White Clouds Moving Upstream, enamel
Stuart Mills

2009

Dirt
Les Coleman

onglet
Simon Cutts

Poems From A Pioneer Museum
Susan Howe

wildflower for Deidre
Simon Cutts, Erica Van Horn

Rosemary plaque, enamel
Erica Van Horn

2010

MATERIALpoetry *
STUDIOpractice

The Book Remembers Everything: The Work of Erica Van Horn
Nancy Kuhl

picodons et pélardons
Simon Cutts

After Brancusi
Erica Van Horn, Simon Cutts

Letters from Brno
Jiří Valoch

tree on the outside
William Minor

with or without
Erica Van Horn

Some More Notes on Writing & Drinking
Bill Culbert, Simon Cutts

2011

Six Jugs
Bill Culbert, Simon Cutts

8 Old Irish potatoes, Living Locally No.17
Erica Van Horn, Simon Cutts

Some More Words For Living Locally, Living Locally No.18
Erica Van Horn,

silk worm box
Erica Van Horn

Mending
Erica Van Horn, Thomas Meyer

the book is the manifestation of the poem / the poem is the manifestation of the book
Simon Cutts

Toscano
William Roth

Affinity *
Simon Cutts

The Windows of St John's Church, Healey, Northhumberland *
Jamie Warde-Aldam, et al

2012

Dubh *
STUDIOpractice

échafaudage
Erica Van Horn

Printed in Norfolk: Coracle Publications 1989-2012 *
Simon Cutts, John Bevis

one
Yoko Terauchi

The A. Goldsworthy Productions 1992-2006
Simon Cutts

Born in Clonmel, Living Locally No.21
Erica Van Horn

2013

51 Drawings
Bill Culbert

The Life of St Anthony of Padua
Erica Van Horn

a line only a word
Simon Cutts

Leftovers In The Work Are The Work
Erica Van Horn

TEA, Living Locally No.25
Erica Van Horn

Brancusi's Sewing Box & other implements 1923-1957
Simon Cutts

Kebab: five silhouettes *
Keith Coventry

A watercolour glass for Marie Bourget
Simon Cutts

CORACLE BIBLIOGRAPHY 155

2014

Stephen Duncalf: The Suburban Fauvist, Little Critic No.20
John Bevis

Mr S Mills visits the Kroller-Muller
Simon Cutts

Modern Dutch Interiors
Erica Van Horn & Simon Cutts

BUS, Living Locally No.29
Erica Van Horn

The Free Music Machine Drawings
Percy Grainger

Some Implications of Poetry *
John Janssen

2015

My Ironmongery
Erica Van Horn

I always have an audience for my work, Living Locally No.31
Erica Van Horn

Natural Cheese, Living Locally No.33
Erica Van Horn

The Window Paintings of Stephen Skidmore, Carpe Diem IV *
John Bevis

aglio 6 olio 2015
Duncan Chappell, Erica Van Horn, Simon Cutts

The Translated Latrine Inscriptions of The Palazzo Davanzati, second edition
Simon Cutts

Construction Storage Despatch
Martin Rogers

The Unit of the Work is the Word *
Simon Cutts

A Short Essay on Ephemera, porcelain version
Simon Cutts

2016

The Pencils of Matsutani
Takesada Matsutani

The Xmas Files
Stephen Duncalf

Brancusi's Sewing Box & Other Works
Catalogue

The Constructed Archive
Simon Cutts

Nymphaes
Simon Cutts

Above
Erica Van Horn

A Mispalcement of Lichen
Erica Van Horn

2017

I prefer the streams of the mountains to the sea
Simon Cutts

In Nannycatch Beck
Simon Cutts & Kate Van Houten

Fly Falls in Milk-jug: The News in Haiku
Maureen Van Horn

When the air is clear
Erica Van Horn

Cork City
Peter Downsbrough

Four Trees
Joan Roth

Peal
Randall Couch

Birdsong
William Roth

An Eye Drop Calendar
Erica Van Horn

Utility Building
Ulrick Ruckreim

A solution is in the room
Maud Cotter

Skylark
Simon Cutts

Selected Postcards 2017
Boxed set

2018

133 Fruit Labels
Erica Van Horn

The Seams of Claude Monet
Simon Cutts

The Balthus Poems
William Minor

Em & Me
Erica Van Horn

Too Raucous for A Chorus
Erica Van Horn, Laurie Clark

The Struggle of the Fly in Marmalade
Simon Cutts

2019

A Slender Horizon of Light
Simon Cutts

Roger Ackling's Furniture
Simon Cutts

Street Signs
Peter Downsbrough

The News in Haiku: Volume II
Maureen Van Horn

I always have an audience for my work 2
Erica Van Horn

A Concertina of Concertinas
Catalogue

Play Book
Maurice Scully

Descriptions of Literature by Gertrude Stein: Handwritten by Erica Van Horn
Gertrude Stein, Erica Van Horn

A Walled Garden: A History of the Spandau Garden in the Time of the Architect Albert Speer
Ian Hamilton Finlay, Ian Gardner

2020	2021	2022
Unique Forms of Continuity in Space Simon Cutts, Maud Cotter	*seasonal words* Harry Gilonis	*picodons & pélardons*, glass version Simon Cutts
Percy Grainger's Dash Simon Cutts	*A Table in Ballybeg* Simon Cutts, Erica Van Horn	*of Lichen & Moss* Erica Van Horn, Kate Van Houten
A Short Essay on Ephemera, glass version Simon Cutts		
Living Locally series 2002-2019 Erica Van Horn